Growing Up in Chickasaw and the Mobile Delta

Ronnie Hyer

Edited by
Vicki J. Barrett

Ronnie Hyer/Vicki J. Barrett

Intellect Publishing

An Intellect Publishing Book

ISBN: 978-1-961485-23-5

First Edition: 2023
FV -8HB

Copyright 2023 Ronnie Hyer & Vicki J. Barrett

All rights reserved. No part of this book may be reproduced in any form or by any electronic, mechanical, or other means now known or hereafter invented, including photocopying or recording, or stored in any information storage or retrieval systems without the express written permission of the publisher, except for newspaper, magazine, or other reviewers who wish to quote brief passages in connection with a review.

Please respect the Author's Rights.

Intellect Publishing, LLC
6581 County Road 32, Suite 1195
Point Clear, AL 36564
www.IntellectPublishing.com

Growing Up in Chickasaw and the Mobile Delta

Table of Contents

ABOUT THE AUTHOR 5
PREFACE 7
INTRODUCTION 9
LIFE IN CHICKASAW 15
    THE BEGINNING… 17
    WALKING TO GRANDMA'S HOUSE… 19
    THE PARK… 21
    THE GREAT GOAT ROUND-UP…!! 24
    CHICKASAW DOGS… 28
    CHICKASAW BABE RUTH LEAGUE… 30
    OFFICER BOOKER… 33
    THE CEMENT DAM…!! 35
    RAT ROCKETS!! 38
    THE SHIPYARD… 41
    SQUIRREL HUNTS… 43
    SQUIRREL HUNTING AND MOONSHINE RICH!! 45
    SKATEBOARD… 48
    THE NEWSPAPER… 50
    BUILDING HUTS… 52
    CHICKASAW ALL BOYS RAILROAD 54
    YOUNCE HARDWARE… 59
    MR. FRANK… 63
    WATERMELON ROASTS… 66
    COLLECTING BOTTLES… 68
    MUSIC AT CAMP CULLEN… 72
    CHATTER BOX… 74
    ROCKET CLUB… 75
    BELLAS HESS AND BOBBY GOLDSBORO… 77
    THE UNLUCKIEST KID I EVER KNEW… 79
THE CAMP 82
    THE CAMP… 84
    UNCLE EMMET… 87
    MEMORIES OF THE CAMP… 90
    TRIPS TO THE CAMP… 92
    THE ALLIGATOR… 94

- Waiting on the log... 98
- The Gunshot... 102
- Helicopter Crash... 107
- The Oil Well... 111

TREASURE HUNTING... 112

- Relics in Chickasaw... 114
- The Air Sho Treasures... 117
- Claurice and Wash... 119
- A Cloverleaf Landing Story... 122
- Ronnie almost dies in Blakeley River... 125
- The Body... 128
- Arrests at Fort Huger... 141

POISONING THE DELTA... 167

- Sad Changes in the Delta... 169
- Polecat Bay... 172

BIBLIOGRAPHY... 174

About the Author

I've known Ronnie Hyer since he was about ten years old. He became close friends with my brother and spent a lot of time at our house while growing up. Ronnie always had an adventurous spirit. He never met a stranger! He had a twinkle in his eye and was always up to something. Everyone who met him loved him and wanted to be part of his escapades. All of us who grew up in Chickasaw at that time were poor by today's standards. We didn't know we were poor because all of us were in the same boat. We were monetarily poor, but rich in friends, family, and adventures.

Ronnie grew up to be a very successful entrepreneur with many thriving businesses both in the U.S. and in Fiji. He was an avid fisherman and historic relic hunter. If he didn't know how or where to do something, he was compelled to figure it out and make it happen. He had a remarkable memory and wrote stories of his life growing up in Chickasaw and the Mobile Delta. His stories were filled with his great sense of humor, leaving the reader with a thirst for more.

In early 2022, Ronnie contacted me and asked me to develop his stories into a book. We met and spoke to each other on many occasions to make sure we were on the same page. I promised to get it to publication. Sadly, Ronnie left this earthly life in his beloved Fiji on July 31, 2023, after an extended illness. He was 72 years old. This book is dedicated to his memory. This is for you, Ronnie! You brought us joy!

With love,
Vicki J. Barrett

Preface

Once upon a time...not so long ago to us that are now in our 60's and 70's....there was a village… They called it Chickasaw. I think they named it after an Indian tribe... I don't know why … but I also don't know why they would name a street after a Yankee general...they just did...

Our parents and grandparents moved to Chickasaw. The ones of us that are now in our 60's, 70's and 80's.

They came from all over, but many were from Prichard and Mobile. All were looking for a quiet place to raise kids. They found it. The perfect place!

They built a Recreation Center. The kids came. There was a pool, basketball, shuffleboard, ping pong and much, much more to keep kids happy and occupied. There was even a HUGE Bar B Que in a separate building for those fund raisers that were regularly held... for one reason or the other.

Those parents and grandparents built a school and beautiful churches in their village. They found the right teachers, preachers, and priests to be sure that the children heard the Word of God...and they took them to church on Sunday... Wonderful churches...

They went on to build ballparks, football fields, and a library. All for the children... not for themselves.

Those early parents and grandparents saw to it that the Village was safe. They built a solid police and fire department and staffed it with the best of men available. The people chosen to run the city and make the decisions were all well respected and went about diligently being sure it was the best Village around. There was a feeling of safety in Chickasaw that I have never felt anywhere else in the world.

Chickasaw was heaven when we grew up there. I do not know of one other village, anywhere, that did such a great job... for the children...

I will be forever grateful to those parents, grandparents and all those wonderful people who made Chickasaw what it was...

Back Then....

HURRAH....HURRAH...HURRAH... to those heroes.!!

Ronnie Hyer

Introduction

History of Chickasaw, Alabama

Chickasaw is a small Alabama town located in east central Mobile County in the Southwest corner of the state. It is about 7 miles north of Mobile, Alabama. It lies on a creek that is a tributary of the Mobile Bay delta region. The history goes back to the time when the area was part of French Louisiana (1702-1763). In 1733 the tract of land, known as the Saint-Louis tract, on which Chickasaw is located, was deeded to John Baptiste Lorandini by his friend, Jean-Baptiste Le Moyne de Bienville, also known as Sieur de Bienville, governor of the territory. Many bands of Indians used the area as crossroads for seasonal migration. Farmers settled in the area, and it later became a trading post. Native Americans referred to the creek running through the area as Chickasas Bogue. The name was later anglicized to Chickasabogue, from which the town derived its name. There is legend describing the use of backwater coves and bayous of the creek as hiding places for pirates. Ferries were used to cross the creek until the construction of a wooden bridge in the early 1900s. Farms and a mill that processed coconuts into oil and soap was in the area in the early twentieth century. The mill was later used to manufacture furniture and wooden equipment.

The actual town of Chickasaw began as a company town. In 1914, at the beginning of World War I, Tennessee Coal, Iron, and Railroad Company (TCI) purchased the land at for shipbuilding (Chickasaw Shipbuilding and Car Company). It was considered suitable because of its position on the North end of Mobile Bay. TCI built the entire town to house workers for the shipyard including stores, community center, health clinic, school, water purification plant, icehouse, sewage treatment plant. The icehouse building would later become a small hospital directed by Dr. C.E. Lange. A total of 14 ships were built and launched there, however, the war ended before the shipyard could be completed. Many workers lost their jobs and left the area.

The shipyard and town were purchased by Mobile businessman, Ben May, who sold them to Gulf Shipbuilding (subsidiary of Waterman Steamship Corp.) in 1938. The shipyard was reopened at the beginning of World War II. Thousands of families moved to the area to participate in the war effort. Between 10,000-15,000 were employed by Gulf Shipbuilding during peak production. The town was expanded into a large community. Updated homes were rented only to workers and others associated with the shipyard. In addition, the Federal Government provided housing in a project called Gulf Holmes, as well as temporary housing structures. Streets were paved. Some of the streets in the town were actually sidewalks with alleys in the rear for traffic to provide safety for young children. A shopping center, with drug store, restaurant, grocery store, and post office were established. Gulf Shipbuilding built 74 ships during the war for the United States Maritime Commission, the United States Navy, and the Royal Navy of the United Kingdom. The shipyard gradually closed at the end of World War II.

Leedy Investment Company purchased the town for 1 million dollars in 1946 and offered the homes for purchase, with priority given to current residents. The townspeople voted to incorporate in 1946 and The City of Chickasaw was established. The former owners donated the disposal plant and parks to the city. City offices were established, and a mayor and 5 councilmen were elected to serve the population of approximately 2,400 citizens. The operating budget was about $60,000. Sales tax, business licenses, building permits, police court, and $1.90 monthly dues to citizens provided funding. Citizens of Chickasaw were a close knit-group with immense pride and interest in their community. The Methodist Church was the first church to organized in 1939 and the building was erected in 1942. This was followed by the First Baptist Church and others. Prior to 1939 religious meetings were held in private homes and the old Playhouse.

Halter Marine reactivated the shipyard to provide tugboats for an increasing offshore industry. Unfortunately, it was closed in 1983 and the shipyard became a small general cargo facility.

Many of the old homes remain in the historic district of the City of Chickasaw, and the area was added to the National Register of Historic Places in 2004.

Ronnie Hyer/Vicki J. Barrett

Growing Up in Chickasaw and the Mobile Delta

Ronnie Hyer/Vicki J. Barrett

Life in Chickasaw

These are my recollections of events that happened to me and my friends while growing up in the wonderful town of Chickasaw. You can't make this stuff up!

Ronnie Hyer/Vicki J. Barrett

The Beginning...

My Grandparents... Melvin Hyer Sr. and Patience Hyer lived at 61 Birmingham Avenue in Prichard. He built that house with his own hands after them moving here from Maine. He helped disassemble an old (even then) paper machine in Rumford Maine and then worked rebuilding that machine on the banks of Chickasabogue Creek in 1929. That machine was still running when they shut the mill down. My grandmother was still washing clothes on a washboard and using a wringer when I was just a kid. That electric wringer was one of the scariest things I ever saw as a kid!! I know she was still washing clothes on that washboard up until the early 60's...

I started life in Prichard, Alabama... like so many of us who wound up growing in Chickasaw. My first memories, as a child, was living on Meaher Avenue. We lived one door away from the Little Store which was right across Meaher Avenue from Prichard Junior High School.... Ronnie (Tree) Dismukes lived across the street.... Mark Shephard lived on the street behind us as did the Lassiter boys... Ronnie's nickname was "Tree"... because he could not say "three"... when he first went to school... He was my best buddy back then and we caught hundreds of crawfish in the ditch behind Prichard Junior High. We moved from Prichard to Chickasaw when I was about ten years old... Chickasaw was awesome. We moved to 217 First Street...right down the street from "The Park" and "The Pool"!! My Dad bought us season passes to the pool that first summer... The pass was a patch that you sewed on to your bathing suit. Me and my sister Lynda were so dang proud of those passes. We could go swimming any day and night we wanted!! It was like going to heaven for kids from Prichard.

We never had A/C in any room in the house when I was a kid.

I also never went to a school that had air conditioning in any room.

The first place in Mobile that I remember having air conditioning was the Downtown Theater. As kids we would ride a bus to town from Chickasaw and just stand by the door at the Downtown Theater to feel the cold air. Never remember having enough money to go inside to see a show.

We were poor in money but rich in adventure...!!

Walking to Grandma's House…

My grandparents remained back in Prichard... and I dearly loved my Grandma and Grandpa... So, I decided to walk back to see them... with my Mamma's blessing... Remember I am about 10 - 11 years old...and this is a good five-mile journey... I did walk to see my Grandma and Grandpa on Birmingham Avenue....regularly...Grandma always had fresh baked cookies and Grandpa always kept a freezer full of Popsicles for the neighborhood kids... BTW...Fudgesicles were my favorite... So, I would go early on a Saturday morning and then return to Chickasaw well before dark....

Early on Saturday I would get up and take off. I would leave my house on First Street...go to Grant Street...then to Court Street... go past the mayor's house and then at the end go up the next section of Court Street... past the house of the prettiest little girl in my world back then...Suzanne Joanna Stein.... and then on to Craft Highway.

Then it was right on Craft Highway..... I might would stop at Gaylords if it was open, and I took a notion.

At the Air Sho Drive Inn sign I would start having to think about spending a bit of the money I had from selling Coke bottles, on ice cream at The Tice Kreme now...or wait until I was coming back home. Usually, the decision was NOW rather than later as you never know just how long you got to live... And missing out on a tall, swirled Tice Kreme soft ice cream in a cone could not be taken lightly.... I usually went in the back door and waited for my delicious treat. Would head back out the same door walking up Craft Highway towards Grandma's house...licking that ice cream as it melted. I would pass the street where the Lejeune's lived and get to what we called Paper Mill Road... Right around there was a business that had a big safe out front with a sign on it...It might have been a pest control company but the safe always impressed me. I wondered why in the world would somebody make a sign out of a perfectly good safe...??

The trip was getting short now...I would pass Montgomery Street where they told me we used to live and then I would get to Coglin's Grocery at the corner of the street behind Grandma's house… took a left...just a few short blocks and I was in for a great day... Grandma had huge fig trees in her yard. She would cook those figs down every year...to make home-made fig preserve stuffed cookies… I loved them… she knew it and always had some ready for me... The last time I talked to her was on her death bed and she promised to have them ready for me in heaven...

Those were good days my friends... very good days...

The Park...

Our little town of Chickasaw was a lot like Mayberry....We even had ole Barney.... We had a very nice recreational park right down the street from my house and across the street from where Stormy Williams lived. I spent many days there playing ping pong, basketball, tennis and watching girls in the Olympic size swimming pool. It never occurred to most of us boys that the pool was there for much of anything else... But we did love to sneak in and swim after it closed…!!

Sneaking into that pool for a swim after it closed at 8 PM..... was almost as good as sneaking into the Air Sho Drive In...in the trunk of a car…!!

Best thing about sneaking in that pool was...no bathing suit was required. Well.... about 9:00 PM one night...not any special night...it was just a night during the summer in Chickasaw... A bunch of us were sitting on the park benches just doing whatever we were doing...anyhow it was decided by most that NOW would be a great time to sneak into the pool. There was at least twenty of us boys. We all went down to the seats at the amphitheater and took off almost all our clothes which was not usually much in the summer...put our shorts and shirts down on the benches leaving us in our underwear to hit the water. Which we soon did... Boy we were having us a big time…!!

Splashing and a hollering and jumping off the high dive... About ten minutes of fun went by and all of sudden somebody yelled COPS...!!! And buddy it was a dang bunch of COPS...!! They come from everywhere to bust up the fun...!!

Guess where I was located when I got the news...?? My underwear only ass was up on the high diving board...!! Boys were running in every direction and the COPS...!! decided it would be great fun to start firing off their pistols to get them to stop...!! Yep, I was in a mess...I had to dive off that high diving board swim to the edge of the pool and then figure out how to not get caught...So I did... I hit the water... two strokes to the edge... got out and then off for the sun deck to jump over the side and high tail it out of there... It was a beautiful plan... The hitch was that Policeman Rollo Jones had picked that exact spot to hide to try to catch one of us. I went over that rail and landed right on top of his head. At that exact split second, he had also fired his pistol up in the air. I never missed a lick... The dang bullet went right up beside me, and my ears were ringing...but I pushed up off his ole head and went back up and over that railing and headed in the other direction. I went over the railing on the other side of that sun deck like Jesse Owens running the Olympic hurdles.... Ran over into the neighborhoods and crawled under a house to hide. Remember I am still in my underwear... it is summer, and this is Chickasaw Alabama... dang mosquitoes ate my ass up...!! I took it as long as I could and then crawled out and went home....

Luckily my parents had guests that night and the only way in was to walk through the whole bunch. I know my parents were proud of their son that night… The COPS…!! had taken all our clothes, of course, and they had to take me to the station to get them... My dad was pissed that they had been firing their weapons, which kinda took the pressure off me a bit… Thank God…!!

I worked with Mr. Jones at the hardware store later on… Never told him that it was me that jumped on his head that night…

It was much better to just laugh about it to myself….

Ronnie Hyer/Vicki J. Barrett

The Great Goat Round-up…!!

The year was 1967... Us boys were 15 -17 years old and all hanging out at The Park... I do not need to name The Park. There were other places for recreation in Chickasaw at that time...but there was only one. "The Park"... Mr. and Mrs. McAdam's ran it ....and we ran them ....crazy! Every single one of us boys loved them both, though. They were our grandparents from another family…

But on this particular day, The Park obviously did not have enough going on to hold our attention.... Time to find something to do...!! When we were younger, Chickasaw had constructed several huge sewage settling ponds back behind Colonel Dixie. They had fenced it all in and put a lot of goats inside to keep the grass mowed. Us being more city boys than country boys...farm animals were very interesting. Not too many of us had ever rode a horse or even been very close to one... There were a few horses somebody kept at the old sewage plant, and we tried to ride them once. Could not catch them so I convinced my buddy to get on top of their stable so I could run the horses by, and he could jump on one just like Roy Rogers would do it.... The jumping on part went well...the landing part did not... my buddy talked a pitch or two higher for a while after that. The getting off part was also a bit troublesome... but my buddy is alive and well today, so no harm done....

So now... about 16 of us took off to the sewage plant to go see the goats... We got there and the gate was locked but the section over the top was open, so we just jumped over it... Started walking around the ponds. It must have been about a mile square with both ponds included. As we would get close to the goats to see them somebody in our group would throw a dang rock at them and they would run... That continued on for a spell... Us walking laughing and carrying on with each other......trying to get close enough to see the goats...

All of a sudden, about three Chickasaw Police Cars roared into the gate of sewage plant. They obviously had a key to the gate...!! We did not run like we most always did, and heck, we weren't doing that much wrong... That was one of our more better days.

The cops pulled up and jumped out all in a huff... They yelled...

"You boys are trespassin!!"... We all kinda looked at each other...like " yeah we are trespassing, but this ain't real trespassing"... We had been cutting through that area for years to go fishing. We said okay, we will leave.... They said... "No sir you all going to jail...!!" We were totally unconcerned and was glad to get the ride honestly...

So, we get to the jail, and they do not even ask us our names. But they did count us... They put us 2-3 to a cell and did not even lock the doors... And NOW is when the fun starts...

The Vigor High School Senior Class President for that year was with us... Now even though Mr. Jerry McNorton was class president he was a cool guy and hung with us of the.... shall I say more adventuresome type...

Jerry was very upset about the current turn of events...and he decided to escape...!! I watched him do it...!! He got down on his hands and knees and crawled out of the cell... down the cell block... all the policemen were in the little booking office... he crawled under the booking desk window so they could not see him, and he was out the door and gone....

So, after a while the policemen decided we had served our sentence and were about to let us go... Till one of them decided to count us...... Right about then all heck broke loose...!!

"What do you mean 15... we counted 16...!!"

Back in the cells we went, except now the doors were locked... This had all been kind of an adventure for me until those dang cell doors were locked... Then it got serious... They were seriously pissed... They would take one of us at a time out to question... trying to find out who escaped... Never got to me... Somebody finally told and they let us all go home...While I was in the cell I was almost wringing my hands... My cell mate Clarence Carrio Jr. went to sleep... I was amazed...

Now... next day in the Mobile Press Register...
BIG NEWS STORY...
"16 Chickasaw Boys Arrested for Molesting Animals"
They made it look like we were trying to do the nasty to dang goats...!! None of us had ever even heard that was

possible... All the cops were from a prior generation and were probably raised on a farm... Craziest thing I had ever heard.... and thought it was funny... We had not been arrested for anything...!!

But for the rest of that school year every time one of us would walk down the halls of Vigor High School... all you would hear was goat and sheep noises... even after Jerry McNorton's Senior Class President graduation speech.... Maaaa...Baaaaaa..Maaaaa..Baaaaa..!!!

Ronnie Hyer/Vicki J. Barrett

Chickasaw Dogs…

Let me tell you about Tobey…and several other Chickasaw dogs… I lived on First Street in Chickasaw, Alabama… In fact, it was 217 First Street… But First Street was not a street. It was a sidewalk. All of the original streets in Chickasaw were built during the "War" …when people who worked in the shipyards worked shift work. First Street was a sidewalk and access was the alley behind the house. Delivery people bringing ice, milk, coal, etc.etc.etc., would not wake up the sleeping shipyard workers… delivering to the back of the house. The Walkers lived next door, Mrs. Faulk lived catercorner from us and Sylvia Burns lived on Second Street where our back yards joined…"Buster" Ervin Nordmann lived next to her…

Tobie was a great dog! He followed me around Chickasaw, everywhere… To the park…to baseball practice, to the Little Store…. across the viaduct…everywhere… I do not remember how Tobey became our dog… He probably just wandered up one day and we started feeding him… That was typically the way you became a dog owner in Chickasaw back then. There were very few pedigree dogs in Chickasaw… All dogs lived outside, and they were nice dogs… None of them bit us .and we all knew the names of those that lived within a few houses of us. Very, very few dogs had to live in a fenced in yard or were ever walked on a leash... We considered that kinda cruel... A dang dog needed to live free... The Carrio's lived just a couple houses away from us on Second Street ...They had two dogs with a real pedigree that you could recognize... They had a bulldog named Pete... I cannot remember the other one's name, but I knew it back then... Pete would bite truck tires for some unknown reason. One morning at the St Thomas School we all went too... we had a outdoor assembly in the morning. Pete had hung around after we all got to school...he had followed us. We were all watching Pete chase the milk truck that delivered milk to the school....as he always did... Well Pete got him a big ole bite of that truck tire that morning and held on.... he went about three times around that tire before he decided he had had enough.......Kerfop..Kerflop..Kerflop......around and around went Petie...!!....we were all screaming....LET GO PETIE..!! LET GO PETIE...!!, but Petie never heard us... He did not get hurt but we sure had a great story to talk about for years to come...

Tobey eventually passed away as all dogs do... he died from heart worms, as I know now.... Dogs never went to the vet back then... We would have never had money for a vet, anyhow...We just loved em, as long as we could, and then cried when they left...

Chickasaw Babe Ruth League...

I participated in the Chickasaw Babe Ruth Baseball League in the middle sixties... Notice I did not say I played in the Babe Ruth League... I just participated. About 1963 several Chickasaw men decided to start a baseball league for the boys. The men I remember involved was J.C. Smallwood, Willard Williams, Stormy Williams and my Dad... Melvin Hyer... There were many more I am sure, but those stand out in my mind. I remember when they chose the Babe Ruth League over the Dixie Youth League... Don't remember why but do remember the discussions...

The first thing they did was build a back-stop in the area where Gulf Homes had been. I think that would be the corner of west Lee and Jackson Street...

So now my Dad is promoting youth baseball so I was expected to play... There were two problems... I had never played baseball...!! Remember I went to St. Thomas Catholic School. We never played hard ball and we never mixed in with the public-school boys that did. We mixed but not in sports...We mixed in jumping in the pool after it closed...building huts.... rail car adventures and other foolishness...but we never played sports together...

So now, I am the only Catholic boy in Babe Ruth Baseball, and I am terrible... Back then coaching was not about coaching...it was about winning... I never remember a coach taking one minute to show me how to do it better... He mostly hit fly balls to the good players...and that was practice... Rickey Bray was our coach that first year, my thirteen-year-old year. Rickey was a great guy, we all liked him, but unfortunately, Ricky is now serving a life sentence for multiple charges of child sex abuse... Of course, nobody is perfect...

We would play against teams from Satsuma and Saraland mainly...Tommie Robinson coached the Braves from Saraland, as I remember....

So, every week we would play a game or two and I would ride the bench...There would be only two of us that never played in a game...even if somebody was sick, we still never played. I think they would rather forfeit the game than play us... But I was okay. I was fulfilling the obligation to my Dad to participate...

One night we were playing the Braves... Something went wrong with our team and they had us 29-0. That was back before they would call a game if it got too one sided... They played it all the way out no matter what...

Finally in the last inning of the game of course after everyone had given up... they looked at me sitting there and put me in as pitcher...as a joke... I knew I was the joke. They were laughing as I walked to the plate...When I started pitching the crowd started laughing. I was left-handed and slow... but you know what...?? I was smiling...I was in the game. The batters knocked me out of the box...but I was still smiling. The game ended and I went home smiling...Later I crawled into my bed and went to sleep smiling...I had been in the game.

I never went back the next year. I was 15, and the smell of perfume and gasoline was now in my system... But that one night in a baseball park in Saraland Alabama... I was a pitcher in the game...

Officer Booker…

Back then… back when Chickasaw was paradise for a younger me… we had a great Police Force. We did not know it at the time, but we were protected by the BEST.

One of them was Officer Booker. Officer Booker was hard on us kids. He did not bend on any situation. He was right down the line. If it was the law, he followed it, and we had to also.

After I had grown up a bit…about 21-22 years old. I was now out of my parents' house. Late at night about 2:00 in the morning my phone rang. Out of a very deep sleep I answered it and Officer Booker was on the other end. He said… "Your family needs you".

Somehow God told me what was wrong… Somebody was severely injured or had died. I asked him… "Who is it?" He repeated… "Your family needs you…" I HAD to KNOW that instant…!! I almost screamed in the phone… "WHO IS IT"… He said "Your Brother"…

I did not say another word. Hung up the phone and headed to Chickasaw. My Brother Ricky had died in a car accident.

I got there to start the process of comforting my family….and myself. Officer Booker stayed with us through the night and into the next morning. He prayed with us.!! He was there for us...!! I will never forget him, and I want everyone to know what a wonderful policeman and asset to Chickasaw he was. His job was not to stay with us… it was simply to deliver a message....

We were devastated, but without Officer Booker there, it would have been worse....

God Bless Officer Booker and all members past, present and future... of the Chickasaw Police Department

The Cement Dam…!!

Back when I was a growing in my hometown… Chickasaw, Alabama… we fished every chance we could. We fished in the ponds of water between, and on both sides of, the railroad tracks. You could catch 100 little bream in a very short time. They had been there, trapped, a long time and were stunted… A big one would be about 4 inches long. We would throw them all back, but they did count in numbers… Somebody asked you "how many fish you caught that day"… you could say 'bout a hunnert' without lying and having to go tell the priest…. I think the rule is that a fisherman can stretch his total catch by about 25% without suffering the everlasting pains of Hell…saw it in the Bible somewhere…

Back to the story….

We fished up and down Chickasabogue Creek…

We fished at Green Water…

We fished at H & W and Petersen's…

Anywhere there was water and fish within walking and later…bicycle distance… we fished.

There was one place we all went to… We called it Cement Dam…!! It was down the railroad tracks on Viaduct Road heading towards Mobile and International Paper Company. Cement Dam was not really a dam…It was the outfall pipe for cooling water from International Paper Company...

That water came out of that pipe in a huge hurry. It was a torrent of very warm water... Catfish loved it...!! You could stand there all day and watch the catfish and gars rolling on the surface of the water... We never caught a lot, but it was our fishing heaven...

One night during the summer we all decided to spend the night at Cement Dam... We got set with the fishing equipment and took off... Please note that I did not say camping equipment, water, or food.... We just took off...

Fished most of the night and as usual we caught nothing.... Towards daylight we figured out the fact that we had brought nothing to eat or drink... About that time, I caught a big ole freshwater eel... I told the guys we were going to eat that thing... Somebody asked how we gonna cook it...?? Hmmmmmm... I'm thinking in my mind... We need fire, a pot, and some water... We had fire, cause we did bring matches... We had plenty of water right there in front of us... Pot... more Hmmmmmmmmm...????? We got a worm can...!! We dumped the worms out on the ground cause eating was now far more important than fishing... I took the old coffee can down to the water and washed it as best I could...filled it half full of water and then put it on the fire... Then we tried to clean that eel without a knife.... That mainly consisted or scraping as much slime off him as we could... with a stick,

Our Maxwell House coffee worm can full of water was now boiling so we curled him down in it.... After a while we was even more hungry, and we decided he was done......and he was. We pulled him out of that can and kinda peeled off the skin... He was soon declared delicious and the best eel we had ever had… Of course, that was the first eel any of us had ever had...but it did hit the spot.... at Cement Dam that morning so dang long ago now...

Rat Rockets!!...

Back when I was a kid and lived in Chickasaw... we were always looking for fun ... Fun usually consisted of an activity that was dangerous, or near likely to get us arrested. One of my good friends came by my house to get me one morning. Probably was a Saturday or in the summer... All other mornings were dedicated to going to school or church. We were members of the congregation at St. Thomas Catholic Church. I was an altar boy...!!... imagine that...!! Well... me and my good friend briefly discussed fishing...swimming...ping pong and other stuff but nothing sounded very exciting...like killing snakes or jumping off the train trestle...so we were stumped...

All of a sudden, my buddy jumped up and said... "Ya' wanna go blow up some rats...!!" and boy howdy did I..!!

I asked where...?? He said behind Chickasaw Drug Store....

All us kids went to Chickasaw Drug Store every chance we got. It was effectively the center of our town. The buses stopped there...Back then a lot of people rode buses... We would sometimes ride the bus to downtown Mobile just to walk around, Chickasaw Drugs always had all the comics books. I knew the exact day every month that the new ones would arrive. They also sold that magic elixir from the gods... A Cherry Coke with ice served in a cone paper cup that fit into a plastic cup holder!! The ultimate concoction on a hot summer day back before air conditioners... I remember it costing 7 cents...

Okay NOW we have a location and a possible rat killing coming up...I asked what we needed... He said we need some gasoline and a stick... Oh my Lord....this is getting better by the minute... Anything that required gasoline and a stick had to be incredible fun... So, we gathered up some decent size weapons and "borrowed" some gas from my Dad's boat and took off... We had to walk through the Park, down across the bridge behind Chickasaw School and then cross the highway... As we walked, he told me the plan of action, Chickasaw Drugs had a place back behind their building where they put their trash... It was not unusual to burn trash back then... They would just let it build up and then set fire to it..

Well, the rats got to knowing where that trash was, and they appreciated them putting it out there... Lots of them came for the feast... They wanted to stay, but there was nowhere for them to hide… So, the rats started digging tunnels to live in... all around that place where they stored and burned their trash....

We got to the back of Chickasaw Drugs and my friend pointed out the holes and they covered about 30 feet by 30 feet... Rat Heaven...!!!

Now we are set for the big rat hunt... My buddy pours about a gallon of gasoline down one of the biggest holes... We sit back and wait for several minutes for all those gas fumes to sink into the lowest levels of the rat condo...

Finally, we pitch a match into that hole and BBBAAAAAARRRRRROOOOOOOMMMMM...!!

Two things happened very fast...First the noise of that blast could be heard all over Chickasaw ..Second...rats were ejected from holes all over that area and in every direction...It was raining rats...!!

Very, very quickly we decided the rat hunt was over...People were coming out of buildings and looking around...Rats running everywhere and two stunned boys holding sticks is what they saw.....We just acted like we was as dumbfounded as they were... Took off running for the woods.....and finally sat down and had ourselves a big ole laugh....That my friends is the ultimate description of fun and adventure for a twelve year old boy back in the day...back in our home town...Chickasaw , Alabama....

The Shipyard…

Growing up in Chickasaw… Boy we had us some good times back then… Viaduct Road ya say.?? I wore out several bicycles on Shipyard Road as we used to call it. Shipyard Road led to the Old Gulf Shipyard. About 15 thousand folks worked there at the Gulf Shipyard during the wars. And they built lots of ships that helped to win those wars. Lots of the old shipyard was left when we were young boys. It drew us like ants to a picnic on a hot summer day. It was right there on Chickasabogue Creek… abandoned. The huge wharves were still there. We would occasionally try to fish there. We called it Long Legs because it had huge long high steel pilings that the wharves were built on… Too dang high off the water for us to really be able to fish… But we went for the adventure more than anything… and there were lots of stuff to get into and explore.

One time we were kinda walking by all the offices that stood straight ahead as you got to the end of Shipyard Road... The doors were all locked or nailed shut. Somehow, we found ourselves inside. I do not remember how it happened...It may have been something to do with space and time and young boys... But somehow, we got to see inside those buildings....

Those buildings were shut down very quickly at the end of World War ll... The calendars on the walls were still on the month everyone left. Paperwork was still sitting on the desks as if that person had just left for lunch and was soon to return...Half empty Coca Cola bottles and coffee cups were on desks. The liquid was gone, but you could see the stain of where it had been... There were huge stacks of IBM cards, everywhere... Most won't remember IBM cards, but that was what provided data to the first computers. They were punched manila-colored cards about 3" x 8" that were fed through a computer... Those offices were like walking into the Twilight Zone...They were sitting there waiting for the people to return... I visited them maybe one more time to show a buddy or two... but I never took anything... I should have... for just memory's sake... A few years later they bulldozed those buildings and hauled it all off to the landfill... I was sick...How could they do that.? I wondered... The buildings themselves were still in great condition...The treasures inside were sacred memories of thousands of people working for a common cause... But it did happen, and it is all now just an old man's memories.... Yes, I grew up in Chickasaw, Alabama...my hometown...

Squirrel Hunts…

When I was a young boy growing up in Chickasaw there were a lot of boys my age growing up at the same time. We reached the age that we could get out but had no wheels. Every young boy loves to fish but we also had no boat within walking distance. The water we could get to on foot was Chickasabogue Creek.

I was very lucky that my Dad had a Camp on Raft River and kept me constantly up the river. But being with your Dad having wonderful days and times did not replace the needed very important skills that a young man must acquire with his buddies

A young boy back then just had to get out there on his own to learn those very important skills like… how to properly spit…how to cuss…smoke his first cigarette… Skills that every man needs to gain at some point in life.

We walked the Upper Chickasabogue, to H&W Beach and Peterson's Landing in Whistler to swim. We would walk to Cement Dam… the outfall pipe for International Paper… to fish close to the mouth of Chickasabogue. That was our walking range… We covered it from beginning to end

One winter we found a boat that somebody let us use. It was docked at the old basket factory near the Chickasabogue Bridge over Highway 43 in Chickasaw.

We used that boat to hunt squirrels further up the creek. One day we were walking home on Highway 43 with about 10 squirrels and a Chickasaw Police Car rolled up on us. Somebody had complained we had been killing them squirrels. It had honestly never occurred to me that anybody did not approve of squirrel stew…but somebody did.

The Policeman admired our catch but then he had to ask. "Where did you boys shoot those squirrels...??"

The border between Chickasaw and Saraland is Chickasabogue Creek. We told him we had got them up the river. He then said… "You boys shot all those squirrels on the Saraland side of the river… right?" Not wanting to lie I started fumbling an answer. He quickly stopped me and told me… "You boys shot all those squirrels in Saraland on the other side of the Creek"…

I said "Yes Sir"…!!!

What a fantastic Policeman… I will never forget that favor.

And from then on, we never shot a squirrel again on the Chickasaw side of Chickasabogue Creek… wink, wink…

Squirrel Hunting and Moonshine Rich!!...

So, we fished and swam in Chickasabogue Creek, from beginning to end... We squirrel hunted it only on the Saraland side. It was illegal to shoot on the Chickasaw side...

I gotta tell you about one squirrel hunting trip we had on Chickasabogue. Sparky Butler and I have been running around buddies since we have been small kids. We got ourselves into several scrapes... through the years... but managed to survive each one somehow... Sparky lived in Whistler and that worked out perfect for us. H & W and Petersons Landing for swimming was closer to Whistler and the fishing and hunting was closer to Chickasaw where I lived.

One winter day we decided that a squirrel hunting trip would be a fine idea... We headed to the basket factory to our borrowed boat. Thinking about it... I do believe that Ervin Nordmann (Buster) owned that boat.

We did get to the boat... We got us, the guns and all we needed in it and paddled up Chickasabogue on the Saraland side... I really have no idea which side, but I throw that in just in case the Statute of Limitations has not expired...

I do believe we shot some squirrels... We always did... Those were fat and happy Bienville Square type squirrels...

On the way back down the river we decided to walk out in the swamp. We parked the boat at what liked like a good stopping place. Then we climbed out of the boat and out into the swamps we went. It was wet and muddy, and I now have no idea what we were trying to accomplish.

We walked maybe 50 yards out and came across a place that had a lot of gallon clear glass bottles kinda covered up with leaves and grass... We ignored them at first, but Sparky tapped one of the bottles with his gun...it broke...!! The smell of alcohol overwhelmed our senses... We had found a moonshiner's stash...!

Now neither one of us drank liquor... but we knew people that did...!! We grabbed up seven bottles as I remember... So far, we were having a productive hunting trip.!!

We got that moonshine and got the heck out of there. I took a bottle to my house. We took the rest to Sparky's house. Before we left my house though we ran into two other friends... Mike Jackson and Johnny McVicar. Of course, we showed then our haul. Since we were now Moonshine rich... we gave them a bottle...

When we got to Sparky's house, we showed his Dad what we had... He got MAD...!! He knew that we coulda got shot and it scared him. But after he calmed down a bit... he decided he needed to take charge of the Moonshine... Being as how we might get shot and we did not want to drink it anyhow... it was fine with us...

Later that night I got back to my house. Me and Sparky may not have wanted to drink that moonshine, but

Mike Jackson and Johnny McVicar sure did...!! They had taken that bottle to Johnny's house and had a party.

Two things happened... Johnny drank so much moonshine his family had to take him to the hospital to have his stomach pumped....

Mike Jackson wound up at the Park... Somebody yelled the cops were coming. Mike took off running and ran head long at full speed into a pine tree and knocked himself out. His sister Vicki Jackson Barrett had to come get him and take him to the hospital...

I kinda laid low in the neighborhood for a while. I did not know if Johnny and Mike might have told where that liquor came from. It was long weeks before I got brave enough to go to either of their houses...

Weeks later I got a message out of the blue from people "in the know" that we better never touch any more moonshine. I took them at their word...

Ronnie Hyer/Vicki J. Barrett

Skateboard...

Back when Mrs. McAdams tried to keep us all straight at the Recreational Center... Back when Chickasaw Policemen, Mr. Rollo Jones, Mr. Frank Jackson, and Mr. Booker... tried to keep us all straight on the streets... Back when having a summer pool pass was so awesome...!! Back when all the girls were pretty, and all the guys were shy...

I loved Chickasaw... I could not wait for Saturdays and summer vacation...we would wake up to another adventure every day.... We lived like Huck Finn and Tom Sawyer...

The Viaduct and Shipyard Road was always a source for adventure... I remember the very first skateboard ever built in the world...well at least in my word...

John Creel took a big ole wood water ski he had found somewhere.... and mounted steel skate wheels underneath it.... WOW...that thing could fly down the Viaduct... And we all did it until, we were too skinned up to do it anymore......The biggest and best hill to ride down was down the Viaduct....You had two choices...You could go down the side that led to Highway 43 and Chickasaw School...and the red light and to almost certain death in the traffic....Or you could take the other side to the Shipyard... or at least where the shipyard used to be...

Now riding it down the middle of the road was not good. The viaduct had concrete sections in it and the road also had big cracks. Also, gravel was always on the road...Those steel wheels were not the right size to get over or through all that... So, the absolute best and safest ride was from the top of the viaduct down the sidewalk...hook a right as you got to the boarding rooms and then on down to the street below... Notice I did not say safe ride…I said "safest". There was absolutely nothing safe about this activity... It would NOT have been ANY fun if it was safe…!!

So... you sat down on the customized water ski...nobody ever stood up...!! You then scooted or somebody pushed you to the point of no return and then you were OFF...!!! 10 milliseconds after that... indescribable terror would set in... You got up speed real fast as you approached that right turn at the bottom of the Viaduct where you had to time that hard lean to the right... exactly right… or you would fly straight off the sidewalk and bodily skid down that gravel filled concrete road....(Note to reader..."not a good thing") Lean too soon, and you might hit the fence and roll head over heels down the sidewalk...(Note to reader… another..."not a good thing")... But should you make it through that section you could then look for a nice long ride to the bottom and to later basking in the adulation from your buddies...

The Newspaper...

My wife and I lived in Mobile for a bit after college in the 90's. She jokes about me, and how I would drive to the Press Register and buy the Sunday Paper right off the press after midnight. My dad taught me that when I was a kid. She says I was such a former jock that I did it because I wanted the sports page and I had to be the only one doing that.

The Sunday Paper was a must have for Mobilians. How did you get yours...hot off the press, street corner paper boys, thrown in front yard or another way?

Lord, I miss the Mobile Press Register... It was once two newspapers. A morning and afternoon edition...

I recently made a very bad financial decision. We have two daily newspapers here in Fiji. Both are very well done, and I read both every day. With the COVID Virus running rampant across this island I decided I needed news faster than running down to the local store or gas station and picking up my newspapers. So, I subscribed to both papers online.!! WHAT A MISTAKE...!! I HATE online newspapers. My Dad, Melvin L. Hyer... My father-in-law, Mr. Emmet Mulvey, and my uncle, Ralph Hyer all worked at the Mobile Press Register. Mr. Emmet and Uncle Ralph did all their life...!! The first thing I have to do when I get to heaven is apologize to all of them.

Let me give you a few reasons why a real newspaper is so much better than reading it online...

First... a newspaper is not just news. A newspaper is a hot cup of coffee early in the morning. It has to do with reading local news and national news WRITTEN and PRINTED by real people. It sets the tone for your day. It makes you decide where you are going to read it. Beautiful cool morning? ... read it out on the patio or pier. No electricity needed. How are you going to work a crossword on the dang computer...?? How are you going to clip those coupons??

Now...once you have read it front to back... what are you going to use to clean fish on...?? I do everything from chopping vegetables to wrapping a sandwich in a newspaper. I am NOW OUT of newspaper to do all that...!! WTH, was I thinking...????

Apologies to my Dad... Mr. Emmet, and Uncle Ralph...

I will soon just start getting my daily news online AND on real paper, and once again, I will enjoy it every dang day...!!

Ronnie Hyer/Vicki J. Barrett

Building Huts...

All Chickasaw boys used to like to walk the railroad tracks... They didn't know why... but they did. I believe it was because railroad tracks always lead to an adventure and clearly, they were the shortest route to get there. Walking railroad tracks was not as easy as a path or paved road due to the ballast stone rocks and the blazing hot steel tracks in the summer. Summer was always the best time to walk the tracks because we were on three months' vacation, and adventure had to be found...!! The rocks provided plenty of ammunition for the occasional snake or bird... The steel rails did provide a smooth but extremely hot surface to walk on if you were wearing shoes but who the heck ever wore shoes in the summer?

Another incredibly awesome adventure for boys was "Building a Hut in the Woods" ...!! We built huts of all sizes and varieties... We built huts underground...on the ground and even up in the trees. The adventure was "building the hut"

I don't remember ever sleeping in "the hut". I remember the underground huts we dug behind the Firestone Tire Store... Pat Creel built a huge one. I worried about being buried alive, so I just checked it out from the outside. We built huts that were awesome... at least to us.

Few would have had held out the rain, but we could sit down inside them and discuss boy things… and that was what was important.

Hut building was a multi-boy (re: gang) activity. You never built a hut by yourself. Just the announcement that we were going to build a hut generated excitement in your gang of friends. We would start as one group, but soon we would split up into smaller groups as there were always some disagreement and questions as to exactly the spot and how were going to build the hut… But huts were always built within about ten foot or so of each other. That way we could keep an eye on each other's progress. Much ado was made about the idiocy of every other hut being built except yours…of course.

Hut building would go on at a frenzied pace for a bit…usually two to three days…and then other adventures would come up. The huts would just sit there and every so often we might go back to take a look at them. We would talk about how incredibly intelligent we were in our decisions and how wonderful our hut was… and of course how dumb all the others were… There probably has not been a hut built in the woods around Chickasaw in years and years, and that in itself… is sad…

Ronnie Hyer/Vicki J. Barrett

Chickasaw All Boys Railroad ...

Us boys had our own railroad...
It all started on the Spur Line... The Spur Line (see Fig.1) was legendary to us young boys... It was where we went for huge, day long adventures. It ran off the East Train Track that ran through Chickasaw. That track was typically the North bound train track... The West track was used for South bound traffic... The Spur Line was an abandoned track that led around to the back of the Old Gulf Shipyard.... It was kinda grown over, but still usable at the time... It was a great open trail for us to hunt for snakes, birds, squirrels. rabbits and anything that

Figure 1

Growing Up in Chickasaw and the Mobile Delta

moved with our BB guns. Never remember us killing much which is good for this story and modern sensitivities...

Some of my friends let me in on the fact that they had "found" a pump style railroad cart... without the pump... It was just a flat cart that fit on the rails and was used for moving material around in The Old Gulf Shipyard... Now it would hold about ten of us at a time... we got it on our Spur Line tracks somehow... it was HEAVY... It had been sitting there in the remains of the Shipyard for a couple decades, but it was still in great shape...

A couple boys could push it until they got to running and then hop on... With the added weight it would pick up speed and go for miles before it stopped.... Get 6 boys pushing it and some would get left behind. It got up good speed fast and you had to pick the exact moment to get aboard... Then we would fly around our whole Spur Line Railroad... We had it going for a couple of weeks and then we decided to build huts on our Spur Line Railroad. We now have about 1.5 miles of railroad track, and we got us a young Chickasaw boy powered rail cart. How in the heck could life get any better for a bunch of kids??... Well, I will tell you how it can get better... We needed huts so we could camp out on the rail line, of course...!!

Normally hut construction was accomplished with whatever minimal materials we could scrounge up nearby. Cardboard was good transportable hut material... Limbs, vines, etc. etc. etc., was always high on the list of easy to obtain hut materials... But this time we had us a railroad cart to bring in materials....and guess what else we had.???. An entire shipyard warehouse full of perfect hut building materials to use...!! We had figured out that since the US Government had not used it in all this time...their fullest intention, all along, had been to give it to us...!!! They had even left us a rail cart to move it...!!

Now as all this fun had been going on... our small little gang of friends had been growing. We now had more friends than we could count. The 6 or 8 of us, that had founded the railroad, had grown to over thirty... So, we picked a great spot right there on the railroad track, and on the bank of Chickasabogue Creek to start hut building... One of the main reasons we picked that particular spot was because there was a likely tree standing there where a rope swing could be set...and we knew exactly where there was a lot of rope...!!

One hut for everyone just would not do. We would never all agree on that...We busted up into small groups and huts started going up everywhere.

It just seemed like the US Government had thought about everything we would need... especially tar paper. Tar paper is the perfect hut building material... A few limbs and a few boards... two rolls of tar paper and you got yourself a fine hut.

We had one-story and two-story huts being built. We had huts on the water and over the water being built... Hut building would go on for a while, and then swimming would go on for a while... The railroad cart now became less fun and hut building and swimming was the new fun...except for the new guys showing up...the end was just beginning for our railroad investment... It had proven to be a huge hit with a lot of Chickasaw boys. Before I could look around, we have been joined by about thirty "new" friends. That was no big deal to us... "the more the merrier" … we thought.

We are now building "hut city" on the banks of Chickasabogue Creek... right on the Old Spur Line. It is in the area of what became "Green Water"... Then it was just woods perfectly designed for boys and huts...We are liberating all the material to build these huts from the warehouses of the Old Gulf Shipyard....Mostly tar paper and a few boards laying around...All a boy ever needed to build the perfect hut......

Now... hut condos are being built everywhere by groups of 2-4 boys all with one central idea but many different variations...

One day we hear some yelling... A group had gone earlier to make a run for material with our rail cart... They came running back into hut city shouting that they were being shot at... Pandemonium broke loose in a huge way… Nobody knew which way to run except just not that way...!!Boys were running off through the woods... jumping out of trees,,, diving and swimming across the creek... some trying to hide and some just running and many swimming... it was PANDEMONIUM at its finest...!!

Me and a few more cooler heads just figured we were caught anyhow and just sat in our partially built huts to see what the heck else better was about to happen...

Directly, two overweight men in suits came huffing and puffing into camp... They said they were Railroad Detectives... I told them that was perfect cause we got us a mystery for sure...Somebody is shooting at our friends...!!

They were very pleased to inform us that that it had been them shooting trying to make the boys with the rail cart stop...Seems they really did not want to run much after boys that day...

Next, they wanted to know where in the heck we got that rail cart... We 'fessed up and told him that the U.S. Government had left it at The Old Gulf Shipyard for us boys to use... They told us that they would not have minded had we of kept it on the Spur Line but over the past week some of our "new" friends had taken it out on the main line for a trip, and that they had almost got run over by a train... We were totally taken by surprise... Seems some our "new friends" had forgotten to mention that to us....

All in all, the Railroad Detectives were okay... Mad cause we made them run but, all in all, okay... They took the rail cart, cause they could not afford to take the chance that would happen again... We understood...

So, the Chickasaw All Boys Railroad came to an end... almost... There are a few of us left with some mighty fun memories...

Younce Hardware…

I knew Younce Hardware from my earliest memories living in Chickasaw. I first remember Younce's when the store was just North of where we all remember it to be. It was located in an old building that looked to be from World War 1 or 2…A big old wood building. I was too young at the time to ever need anything from the hardware store, but it was an adventure to stop and just peek around inside. Mr. Younce and another man named Marshall would keep a close eye on ya'… Marshall Tew… worked for Mr. Younce for many years. Eventually Mr. Younce's daughter married a man from Jones County Mississippi named Jim Breazeale who also went to work at the store. Mr. Marshall Tew left Younce's about the time they moved to the new store. He went into the Plumbing business which became very successful… This was all in the late 50's and very early sixties… Back before those apartments behind this location were built… Back when the Bodden's bought the old barracks and turned them into rooms to rent out… Back when Mr. Becker opened his sporting goods store next to Mrs. Williams' grocery store. Mrs. Williams was Donnie and Stormy's mother… Back when I was about in the 4th or 5th grade across the highway at St. Thomas Catholic School.

The ditch that runs under the highway at that location used to flood in any big rainfall. I am sure Mr. Younce had many problems with flooding at this location. Eventually the City or somebody straightened it out to improve the drainage...

When I would peek in Younce's back then, in the old building, I remember big stacks of feed and a big ole dark building filled with interesting stuff to look at...... I loved it...little did I know that I would start a life journey there just a few years later...

As we grew up us boys that lived in my neighborhood in Chickasaw always went up to the Curb Market and hung out. It was the place to go to get a coke and a candy bar and just sit outside and talk... Wilmer Smith owned the Curb Market and put up with us sitting around outside plotting our next adventure.

How did I get the job...?? Well, I was 16 years old and a Sophomore at Vigor High School...I had already been asked not to return to McGill Institute by the Jesuit Brothers. So, to Vigor I went where all my friends were, anyhow. The Brothers must have thought I would do better in a school with more girls, as that is all I seemed to care about...

One day Jim Breazeale.... who was Mr. Younce's son in law... needed some help cleaning out their warehouse. He called Mr. Smith and asked if any of those boys were hanging around, and if so, send up two of them to work a day... Mr. Smith picked myself and Pat Creel to send up there... We both worked like animals that day, moving feed and fertilizer and all else around and sweeping under it. I remember that day so well Pat...

Jim called me in later and asked me if I wanted a regular job... Hours were 6:30 till 7:30 before school sweeping floors. After school from 3:30 till 5:00, and all-day Saturday... I was over the moon and quickly accepted... I had landed a real dream job as far as I was concerned... That started a transformation in my life that has carried me through all these years. I can never thank Jim Breazeale enough for giving me that job

My salary was $60.00 per week. Payday was Friday. After a little while, Mr. Younce changed my payday to Saturday. He explained that I seemed to not be as worn out on Saturday if I did not have that money in my pocket on Friday night to go out and chase girls... he was a very smart man.

I would arrive every morning at 6:30 A.M. My first job was to take a dust mop and sweep up and down each aisle of the store. The dust mop was not as wide as the aisle, so each aisle took two passes. You would shake the dust mop at the end of the aisle...and then come back with a regular broom and dust pan to get it all up... That would take most of the hour. Then I would tidy up the other areas... and take out all the trash. Finally, before I left, I had to take care of the Iguana's. Mr Younce was a real master at putting things in the store that people wanted to come see. From his antique collection in the back, to the iguanas..., it was there to entertain, educate, or just scare the wits out of folks...

Ronnie Hyer/Vicki J. Barrett

The iguanas were a main attraction... I fed them every morning. They ate lettuce almost exclusively. I also made sure their cage was clean. We put 36" wide brown paper, from off a roll, in the cage... which had to be changed regularly. If not, the cage would smell... I never let it get dirty and smell as long as I was there. I also had to make sure they had water… The iguanas were completely docile... The only thing they might do is scratch you, unintentionally, if you had to move them to clean the cage… I sometimes felt sorry for them being caged up, but as long as we fed them, and kept the water coming, they never complained.

Mr. Frank...

This really happened a long time ago in the little town I grew up in....The names will be changed to protect the guilty... This is not as it happened exactly, but as I remember it... and it is very close to the truth...

Chickasaw greatly resembled Mayberry... We had a barber shop and a sheriff's office and all those things that make it so charming and so Southern...and yes, we even had a few town drunks...

Well.... we had us a First Baptist Church. In fact, it was called The Chickasaw First Baptist Church and nobody ever questioned whether it really was or not. It had by far the largest congregation in our little town.

Our police chief's name was Frank Johnson... Him and his wife, and his secretary Miss Carol Bigbosoms, all went to The Chickasaw First Baptist Church as was right and holy.... I worked at the hardware store and was about 16 or 17 years old. Now the local hardware store sold all types of things that could fix just about anything in your house... and feed, seed fertilizer, and everything else you would find in old time hardware store... The hardware store was owned by a man that was considered wise and a longtime member of The First Baptist...so when the

Church had serious problems, the church men would congregate at the hardware store to figure it out...

Now on one Sunday... not any special Sunday... just a Sunday... the church service was going strong... All of a sudden, out of nowhere, our Police Chief... Mr. Frank Johnson stands up and stops the service... He then tells everyone attending The Chickasaw First Baptist Church that morning, that the LORD had spoken to him that week...!!! Well... I can guarantee you... you could hear a pin drop in the Church... something like the LORD speaking to our Police Chief, Mr. Frank Johnson, just did not happen on a regular basis... He continued on to tell everyone that the LORD had commanded him to leave his wife of many years and MARRY his secretary Miss Carol Bigbosoms...!!! You could continue to hear a pin drop after he said it... He added that he hoped everyone understood he had to do what the Lord had commanded him to do, and hoped he had the blessing of the Church... After the Church was over everyone went home the phone switchboards lit up...... I can imagine the conversations...

Margaret: "How do you feel about it, Mary?"...

Mary: "Well the Lord did talk to him"...

And so, it went on through the day and night until Monday morning. On Monday morning, all the church men gathered at the hardware store to figure out how to handle the situation... I was there with 'em, working in the hardware store...

Ol' Frank had 'em in a tight spot... Normally, when a middle-aged guy like him does something like Frank just did... he had to go... but he WAS the Police Chief...!! AND

Frank had called on the Lord as his reason for doing it... So, there was a lot of head scratching and chin rubbing going on...

I walked by at one point, and they all looked very puzzled... I offered my opinion... I told them this...

"Gentlemen... I really don't think it was the Lord a talking to Mr. Frank Johnson our Police Chief...

I think it was them big ole titties a talkin' to him...!!"

That broke up the meeting for the day.

Watermelon Roasts...

So dang many good memories from those days...back then...in my hometown of Chickasaw, Alabama...

I have often wondered if other areas enjoyed a Watermelon Roast as much as we did back in the day... at Vigor High School. We would usually have one after a big football game or school dance. I, so fondly remember the watermelon roasts at what we called H & W back then. I think they call it Chickasabogue Park now... It is a gorgeous beach on a bend in Chickasabogue Creek, way up where it begins... The water is cold, clear, and fresh... Back then it was not easy to get there...

We had to drive all the way around through Whistler to Aldock Road... Almost no one would ever be around especially after dark. Perfect place for a huge watermelon roast.

A Friday or Saturday night would be selected. Sometime in the week before we would find the hugest watermelon around...

Us boys would get our girlfriends...there would be about twelve couples....

Somebody would get out there early and start the fire on the beach. By the time all the couples got there it would be roaring...... it would be the darkest of night.... Once we knew everyone was there... and the timing was perfect... We would toss that big ole watermelon in the fire...

Soon as it exploded... all the couples would run out in the woods and get 'em a piece....

AHHH...wonderful memories from back in the day......

Ronnie Hyer/Vicki J. Barrett

Collecting Bottles...

Back before I became very interested in old bottles and Civil War relics...my interest in bottles were that you could sell them for 4 cents each. And back then in Chickasaw 4 cents got you well on your way to a candy bar and Coke.... I never remember asking my parents for money for such frivolities... But I was pretty dang good at figuring out a way to get to enjoy those finer things in life as a kid... Hunting for coke bottles as we called them was probably the fastest way to get cash together there was, during those days. It was also much like treasure hunting... Back before the "Don't Be a Litterbug" campaigns folks would just toss or leave coke bottles everywhere... We would ride our bikes or walk... first up and down Highway 43... Searching one side of the Highway on the way to Chickasabogue Creek... then on the other side on the way back. That trip alone would usually net enough for the basics... We would sell them at Delchamps where Mr. Fred Denton was the manager, or later on, to Mr. Wilmer Smith who owned the little grocery store next to Beck's Sporting Goods...

But on some days, we would not have as much luck as we needed, or just had a bigger adventure in mind... Like maybe catching the bus at Chickasaw Drugs for a full day of running around downtown Mobile... Now THOSE were some real adventuresome days...

So, we would expand our coke bottle treasure hunt... We could decide to head up Highway 43 to Telegraph Road towards Mobile, or we could go by the Air Show Drive In towards downtown Prichard...

On this one particular day, we had gone behind the China Doll Rice Company across those tracks and had walked the earliest streets ever built in Chickasaw. When the idea of the town of Chickasaw was first conceived it was to provide homes for the original workers in the Old Gulf Shipyard during World War I... A company was put together... homes built, and construction was started on some concrete boats.... Unfortunately, the War ended too soon for them... The company and people languished until World War II and by then they were ready and took a huge part in ship production in that war....

We had been back in that very oldest area of Chickasaw that is kinda where the Honeywell / Union Carbide Plant is now. We had walked those streets. They were old dark, overgrown, and very spooky to young boys... The one thing that I remember about it, besides how spooky it was, is that there were very, very old coke bottles everywhere...!! These bottles were twice as thick and heavy as the current ones, but we thought we might see if we could sell them... On that particular day, we loaded us up all we could carry… Seeing that Delchamps was the closest buyer we headed to see Mr. Denton... who would not take them. Discouraged we went to see Mr. Smith who did buy all of them for 4 cents each. It later turned out that Mr. Smith was a very early bottle collector and realized how much these very early soda bottles were worth... We were just happy to find somebody fool enough to give us 4 cents each...

Here are a couple of the earliest Chickasaw maps I can find of that area... If you remember the Go Kart track on Wilson Avenue behind the Tice Kreme... this area included all of that... Notice on the 1930 map that the Mobile Light Railway ran all the way out to Chickasaw. That was the Streetcar track... I never knew that it did....

I have always searched for what others discard. If I need a chain, I go to the scrap metal yard and search around... Even if I do not find the chain that I wanted I will find something that I cannot leave without. I have always been that way. Might be why I have been metal detecting for 53 years now. Back when I was an outside office supply salesman for Waller Brothers Office Supply... I had the Downtown Mobile territory. One day I was walking from one account to another, and they had torn up the sidewalk. A trench had been dug about 6 foot deep under the sidewalk area... I had on the required coat and tie of that period, and as I passed by the trench, I saw very old bottles falling out of the side. I am also an old bottle collector. I walked past those bottles and saw some good ones... I walked to the corner...turned around and walked back by, looking again. On the third pass I could not stand it anymore. I leaped down into that muddy trench and started grabbing every good bottle I saw. I filled my pants pockets... my jacket pockets, and even my shirt pocket with beautiful, to me, muddy 100-year-old bottles... Yes, people were looking as I climbed my now muddy ass out of there with those old bottles. I just acted like it was a regular day and walked to find my car... and stashed the loot...!!

Ronnie Hyer/Vicki J. Barrett

Music at Camp Cullen...

Back in Chickasaw... back then when life was good... I had a circle of friends that included folks of all types. I want to tell you about a weekend we had... back then. The three friends I remember that were there were Chipper McVicar... Johnnie McVicar and Mike Jackson... We had all gotten an invite to play music for a group of kids from Birmingham at Camp Cullen in Daphne... Now I have no idea how we got the invite... Johnnie played drums and we all kinda sang along... I can't remember who else played an instrument, but who the heck cared...!! We was a band and had a gig...!! Chipper was the oldest... by far the craziest of all of us... and he had a driver's license...! So, we took off to Daphne on a Friday night. Chipper decides we have hit the big time, and we need a bottle of whiskey... Probably my first time ever drinking the hard stuff...

We get there... set up, and the band starts playing... now this group of Catholic kids turn out to be our ages...!! And it mainly consisted of very nice and very good-looking girls... Nobody danced for a spell... but after a few trips to the car for a sip... I DECIDE that I am the best dancer in the world, and get it started... I remember at one point dancing with the whole room. We set them on fire, and EVERYONE was having a blast... but I kept going to the car for a sip too many... The chaperones finally inform us that they smelled whiskey and to finish it up... We obliged...

Chipper had come up with our accommodations for the night... Sleeping in holes in the sand at Gulf Shores on the Beach... We headed to Gulf Shores... which turned in to another adventure... for another time....

Mike Jackson and I have remained friends through all these years... Chipper and Johnnie soon moved to Pensacola. Chipper died a few years back... The last time I ran in to him was in a fast-food restaurant in Mobile. I walked up to him and said, "Hi Chipper...!!" He looked at me like I was crazy and said… " Shhhh, I'm wanted in 6 states"... and that was the last I ever saw of him...

Good, bad, or indifferent... it is a weekend I will always remember... thanks to a wonderful group of friends... back then... in Chickasaw, Alabama...

Ronnie Hyer/Vicki J. Barrett

Chatter Box...

The Chatterbox - To the guys I hung out with back then...The Chatterbox was legendary. Guys like Chipper McVicar, Johnny McVicar, Mike Jackson, Kenneth Carrio, Clarence Carrio (Junior), Tommie Necaise, Joe Hilbert, Buddy Carlisle, Tommie Ferguson, Ervin Nordmann, Donnie Carlisle, Keith Moseley, John Selman and so many more... We would all kinda' go separate ways on Friday and Saturday night... but we would all show up at the Chatterbox sometime after 11:00 P.M. to midnight.

We would order coffee or maybe a Chatterburger and just jump in the middle of a dozen different conversations going on all around us... So many good times there. We had a waitress we called Moon Maid and they seemed to love us all. I think the waitresses and the owner enjoyed it as much as we did.

We might have gone to a football game, a Dance, out on a date or to Mississippi to buy beer. 14 was the legal age in Mississippi to buy beer back then. No matter where you went it was mandatory to meet at The Chatterbox after the night was over... There was never a place like the Chatterbox. I swear it was like Happy Days just a few years later....

Rocket Club...

Remember the Rocket Club in Prichard.??. I pulled up to it at the light across the street... on Paper Mill Road at Telegraph Road... one morning on the way to work. All of a sudden, the front door swings open, and two guys tumble out fighting... Wow... I think to myself... this is going to get interesting.!! A woman staggers out the door behind them... She looks like she has spent the last 40-50 years on a bar stool. She is screaming and I realize they are fighting over her.!! Well, the fight escalates. They both bring out knives and start swinging ang gigging at each other... I see no blood, but one decides he has had enough knife fighting fun and crawls under a car. Now the other one starts running round and around the car trying to stick the guy under the car...He runs to one side... guy under the car crawls to the other side... Bar lady is still screaming... After just a bit, Prichard Police shows up. They get the guy out from under the car and take the knives away from both of them... Then they put both of them in the back seat of the Police Car...!! And those two then proceed to beat the crap out of each other in the back of the Police Car.!!! The cops just kinda watched and let them get it all out... waited for it to settle down and then took them to jail. Bar lady goes back inside to her bar stool.

Ronnie Hyer/Vicki J. Barrett

I drive on to work thinking… "What a great day this is going to be…!!"

Growing Up in Chickasaw and the Mobile Delta

Bellas Hess and Bobby Goldsboro...

I was at the Grand Opening of the Bellas Hess shopping center. It was on Azalea Road at Airport Boulevard. Bellas Hess was a huge deal when it opened... Their big unique feature was that your groceries were delivered to you outside on a roller conveyor... Turned out that the conveyor made almost no sense and was soon abandoned. Bellas Hess was the first store in Mobile that had other stores inside... they called 'em departments. It even had a gun department. To us that were there....it was a HUGE advance...!! Looking back today it was just a medium size store with groceries coming out on metal rollers.

My almost single memory of the entire event was a tent outside where people were waiting to see this young performer... I was young...maybe 11. Somehow, I got away from my parents and wiggled my way right up-front right by the microphone... This was not a huge tent... maybe had about 75 people in it all standing up... No chairs... Microphone was on a small piece of old carpet on the asphalt pavement parking lot...

All of a sudden, in comes this young man. He was such a pretty, nice person... Had I of ever had any homosexual tendencies, I would have been in love. He was beautiful... I did not know his name and there was no announcement made... I was right beside him looking up in awe... He opened his mouth and I had never heard then or since more beautiful music... That is all I remember... but I was there, at that new Bellas Hess shopping center, in that little tent... in that asphalt parking lot.... back then...to hear that young man from Marianna, Florida at the very beginning of a later highly successful career... sing his music... Mr. Bobby Goldsboro

The unluckiest kid I ever knew....

I had a friend when I was young...very young. We were about the same age. He was adopted by his parents. He lived on the other side of town from me. I knew him because his Dad worked with my Dad.

We knew each other from before we have memories. Sometimes we saw each other when his Dad came up to the camp on Raft River. We would get to spend some time together.

As he grew, I noticed that he never moved without his Dad's approval. He sat in his spot on the boat and never said much. His Dad never let him drive the boat that I am aware of.

My Dad had me driving the boat from a very early age. Driving the boat with him in it at about age 8... Soon I was running the boat by myself at age 10-12 on excursions to Chuckfee Bay, up Oak Bayou and even to Gravine Island later... Not my friend...ever.

One day at the camp his Dad came back with a huge beaver tail. He brought it in to tell his story of killing the beaver in the middle of the river. My Dad asked "All you took was the tail…?? with a disgusted look.

We never killed anything we were not going to use for food. I could tell my friend.... the unluckiest kid in the world.... was not impressed either. But he said nothing.

At one point I started spending the night with my friend. I did a few times...not many...it was stressful.

One night I had taken a bath and walked back into their living room. I started to sit down on a green plastic Naugahyde recliner. All of a sudden, my friends mother let out a blood curdling scream.... and a yell... STOP...!!!! she started almost crying saying... "He was going to sit down in our chair WET...!!!" Apparently, I had not dried my back to her liking.

It went on for several minutes with her blubbering about the tragedy the that "almost just happened"... I had never seen anybody act like that in my life...!! I was about 8 at the time.

The next day my friend and I were out in the back yard doing something fun. Can't remember what it was but soon it had to come to a quick stop.

The story was that this family had went to see a neighbors son play an accordion several weeks before. Oh Boy they loved it and their neighbors were proud of their son.

My friend made the mistake of telling his parents that he also would like to play the accordion... Ohh Boy!! ... his parents were excited... Soon they would have other neighbors over to see my friend, their son, play the accordion also.

Problem was that my friend had said that only to try to make them proud of him. The accordion practice quickly became a chore...

My friend's Dad was not as easily deterred from the dream of impressing neighbors with his accordion playing son…

That accordion cost a lot of money and his son was going to practice every day until he could play it as well as their neighbors son.

Our play time ended with his Dad stepping outside with a belt in his hand and wearing a wife beater tee shirt. My friend started crying almost immediately… He was drug in the house with me following. Sat in a chair and the accordion hung around his neck. Next began 30 minutes of him squalling and his Dad wailing the heck out of him with a belt… while at the same time screaming at him that he asked for the accordion and By God he was gonna practice… I don't think my friend ever learned much accordion…

Later we never saw each other much. Life went on…

I saw my friend a few times for brief moments… He had become an alcoholic. He later died from alcoholism.

I understood… He never had a chance….

Ronnie Hyer/Vicki J. Barrett

The Camp

My Dad and his friends built a nice camp for us on Raft River in the Mobile Delta. We had wonderful adventures there! The following stories are just some of those adventures. Great times!

Growing Up in Chickasaw and the Mobile Delta

Ronnie Hyer/Vicki J. Barrett

The Camp...

My Grandfather, Melvin Hyer Sr., moved his family down from Maine in 1929. He came here to work reassembling an old paper machine on the banks of the Chickasabouge River. That old paper machine was the beginning of International Paper Company. It was still running when the plant was closed a few years back. Grandpa fell in love with the area... especially for the fishing and hunting. His sons, Melvin Jr. my Dad, and Ralph my uncle, grew up fishing and hunting the delta.

My Dad married Dorothy (Dot). They had five kids... Me, Lynda, Ricky, Colleen Hyer Kennedy, and Pamela Ann... We also grew up in that same fashion.

In about 1963, my Dad decided to build a camp house on the Delta. He got in touch with Francis Meaher... the caretaker of most of the delta for the Meaher family. Francis took him to see a spot on the island in the middle of Raft River near the head of Crab Creek. Dad leased the property (see Fig.2) and proceeded to build a very nice camp. It became a project that involved most of the Pressroom at the Mobile Press Register where he worked, and of course, Dot and all the kids. Dad had a 12-foot Stauter wood boat with an 18 HP Evinrude. He hauled us and all the lumber, nails, windows, pilings and groceries back and forth day after day for days, weeks, and months. When it got to the point that we could stay overnight it was a wonderful place for us kids... and all his friends.

We could fish off the wharf or just have an adventure poking around in the swamp... So many adventures that this story could go on for days.

One of the things that we had to eradicate first was all the water moccasins. They were everywhere. I now think it was because we caught a lot of fish and cleaned them out on that wharf almost every day. Snakes love to eat fish or left-over fish parts...

Our family grew up there at The Camp...only name it ever had... We are now almost all gone with most now in heaven and the few left waiting to join them... We loved that camp and were so lucky we had a Dad that made our life an adventure...

Names I need to mention that were part of that build and the adventures that followed are...

Mr. Emmet J. Mulvey (my father-in-law)

Mr. Billy Schemmer.

Mr. Nick Shamp

Mr. J. C. Hudson

Mr. Stringfellow

There were more. Several more and I apologize to those I have missed.

Ronnie Hyer/Vicki J. Barrett

Figure 2

Uncle Emmet...

When I was about three years old, I learned I had an Uncle Emmet. He was not my real uncle, but he was my Dad's best friend. He was Uncle Emmet, and his wife was Aunt Jackie to all of us kids.

It was common for kids to call their dad's friends uncle back then.

Emmet J. Mulvey was always the greatest man I knew and still is to this day. Uncle Emmet worked with my Dad at the Mobile Press Register. They were both Pressmen. They printed the newspaper. They worked at night printing the morning newspaper. The Mobile Register. The afternoon paper was the Mobile Press, and it was printed in the daytime.

Uncle Emmet was the life of the party everywhere he went. If you knew him or ever met him... you remember him.

He and my Dad were partners in the catfish netting operation. They owned about 25-35 gill nets over time.

My Dad did most of the putting out and running the nets. I was not a partner, but it became my job to pick the weeds and trash out of the nets when they were brought home to clean and bleach. These were nylon nets, and a bit of grass would always hang up on every single knot It was my job to hang the net up to dry and then remove that bit of grass. The nets had to be hosed down and bleached also.

If the net was loaded with mud and dirt or grass the fish would not hit them.

Uncle Emmet always gave a name to some people he really liked... and sometimes it would stick. His wife Jackie became Momma Goose. If he spoke about her, he said "Momma Goose" and everybody knew exactly who he was talking about.

My Dad Melvin became "Gummy". Dad had all his upper teeth removed and wore false teeth. Hence "Gummy".

Emmet would call our office and ask to speak to "Gummy" even years later. We would have to tell new employees who Gummy was.

Uncle Emmet gave me a name for a couple years...

My Dad and I were in his Stauter boat running nets one day. Emmet was in his Stauter boat running nets also. I was I guess about 10-12 years old. Dad was letting me run the boat. The boat had an 18HP Evinrude on the back. The one thing I had been exposed to was how my Dad and Emmet would run fast through the ditches. They knew the area and the boat and motor. I did not and was just learning how to run the boat.

On the way back to the causeway we had to run in to Roundtree's Ditch. Dad was keeping his boat there at Roundtree's. We were in front of Uncle Emmett, and I decided that the race was on. I rounded one corner fine... but at the next corner I suddenly forgot which way the throttle turned. I hit the gas instead of slowing down in the turn. The Stauter boat hit the bank in the turn, and we went all the way up on the bank out of the water. My dad was laughing but nothing could have been worse than Uncle Emmet coming round that corner behind us. He saw what had happened and almost hurt himself laughing.

From that day, and for about two years, my new name became "Dry Land Sailor". Oh Lord I hated that, and was so glad when it finally went away...

Memories of the Camp…

Many nights I would lay awake in bed listening to my Dad and all the men telling stories at the camp. Some nights they would have gone by to see Clovice at his place on Blakeley River. Clovice sold shinny. Those nights the stories and the laughter would get a lot louder. I would go to sleep laughing myself to death.

We slept under very heavy blankets at the camp. The night could be freezing cold and all you needed was one of those blankets and you were toasty warm. I figured out later in life where those blankets came from. They were repurposed from wool felt conveyor belts from International Paper where my Grandpa was Superintendent of the bag plant.

Once my Dad and his buddies came into possession of a military field phone… My Dad and all the guys were very sure to obey the seasons and almost all of the limits but… if they might find a way to bend the rules just a bit… they might give it a go…

A military field phone back then was a way to catch catfish… When you crank the phone, it generates electricity. Stick the wires in the water and it would shock a catfish and make him come to the top. My Dad hated the guys who used a telephone to shock catfish. But since they now had one… they had to give it a try.

Him and Emmett tried it out in the river… No luck… they did not know how to use it… but it did make for several funny stories about how scared they were just having it in the boat.

Once they got it back to the camp… they figured out that if you hooked it up to that brass doorknob on the camp it would shock the crap out of whoever was coming in the door… That made it worth all that worry about having it… It was highly illegal to even have one in possession in the delta…

A week or two later after a trip to Clovice's, and a few drinks… Emmett decided that he had worried about that damn phone enough.

He grabbed it up… walked out to the end of the wharf and pitched out into the middle of Raft River… Never to be seen or worried over again…

Ronnie Hyer/Vicki J. Barrett

Trips to the Camp…

My family spent a lot of time up at The Camp. Summertime, Spring Winter, and Summer.

We would all pile in the 1956 Chevrolet Bel Air V8 and head to the causeway. First, we loaded the car with gallon jugs of drinking water. Glass jugs not plastic. That was all the water we would have for the entire trip. The 12 Foot Stauter with the 18HP Evinrude was towed behind the car. There would be at least five of us kids and Mom and Dad. Maybe a friend or two got invited along also.

First, we had to stop at the icehouse in Prichard. We would buy two blocks of ice… One for the refrigerator at the camp and one for the fish. We never carried cokes or any soft drinks along. That was an unthinkable luxury in those days.

Next stop was to fill up the boat, and that would probably be at the Hudson Station on the Causeway that always had the cheapest gas around. The Evinrude being a 2-stroke engine, Dad had to add oil to the gas. He always bought bulk oil in the glass bottles with the metal spout kept at the service stations. Bulk oil was a mixture of what came out of the regular oil cans. It was whatever was left in the bottom of those cans… and it was cheap. The motor ran on it, and that was all that Dad required.

Next stop was usually Bensons Bait Shop for a visit, and then a launch at either Roundtrees or Billy and Quennie's shop across the river.

We would pile all that in that 12-foot Stauter boat and head up the river...

Up Tensas River to Upper Crab Creek... Crab Creek to Raft River, then a right to get around the point of the island... Left, like you are going to Oak Bayou, and then The Camp was right there on the left on the island... Then the good times would begin...!!

I had to get you there, before more stories could begin...

The Alligator…

This takes place about 1962… give or take a bit. Dad and his buddies are moving along on the construction of the camp. It is summertime. The spot has been cleared. The creosote poles have been sunk into the mud, 2" x 8" mud sills have nailed to them at ground level to keep them from sinking any further.

Now they were putting in the framing for the floor and nailing down the floors.

Billy Schemmer had come up to help Dad that day and I brought along a buddy… Buster Nordman. Busters real name was Ervin but us boys only knew him as Buster… back then.

As we took that left into Raft River, we noticed a pretty good catfish that was floating on a trot line. Somebody had put out a trotline and then left it. The fish on the line had died and floated to the top. We did not stop. My Dad would never touch somebody's fishing lines. Even if we did see a huge fish on a limb line, we would never mess with it. He hated folks who would run your lines or nets. He had a lot of that happen to him back then, but he would never even consider stealing fish.

So, we pulled into The Camp. Unloaded the lumber and Dad and Billy went to work.

Again... it was summertime. There was no wind, and it was blazing hot. Not much for me and Buster to do but sit and sweat. I have no idea how Dad and Billy was working like they were.

After a bit, Buster and I decide to go swimming. We dove in and was swimming in the river. Back and forth we would dive in... get out and dive again.

We soon notice that a big log is floating up the river. It had come around the bend and was kinda getting close.

I got a little worried and went and told Dad. He was nailing down floorboards. He just looked over his shoulder and said we were alright. It was just a log.

We went back in... The log kept getting closer. I went back and asked Dad if logs floated upstream... That got his attention...

There were not many alligators back then. We never saw them in the day. We would see them at night when frog gigging.

It seems to me that our current alligator population exploded after the Nutria had eaten all the grass roots and then became alligator bait. Nutria now have a tough time surviving. Alligators love it and the population is now beyond my belief.

So, Dad looked again at the log and realized it was a huge alligator (see Fig.3). Billy went to his boat to get his 22 rifle to run the alligator off. He shot at him several times. The gator would go down for a few minutes but persistently he would come back up trying to get past the camp.

Figure 3

Billy would pop a few rounds in his direction. He was not trying to kill the gator… we just wanted him to move on. One more time Billy takes a shot to make him go and the gator goes completely berserk. He starts spinning at 100 MPH.!! He is thrashing and throwing water high in the air.

When it finally stopped… me and Buster decided we done had all the swimming we needed for that day… Dang that was scary…

Here is what we figured out later. That gator was after those catfish that were floating on the trot line just past the camp. Being obviously hungry he might have settled for a tasty white boy in the meantime.

Billy had hit that gator right in the eye with the 22. He did not mean to kill him. We were taught to never hurt or kill anything that we were not going to eat. And that was the rule at the camp.

We found that gator the next week on the bank in Crab Creek. He was impressive. Biggest alligator I have ever seen anywhere... even on TV. It was a good adventure.

Ronnie Hyer/Vicki J. Barrett

Waiting on the log...

The year was 1962... it was warm, so probably it was early spring. Our entire family had been up to The Camp all weekend. I am sure I remember some of what happened that weekend but gradually the memories all run together. It is hard to separate them into days or weekends now... I have to tell you the events without connection to a timeline. Hope you understand.

This event was all of us packed in that 12' Stauter boat with an 18 HP Evinrude. The weekend was over... Dad needed to get back home to get ready to work that night at the Mobile Press Register. It had been a nice day, but in the afternoon, it had gotten a bit stormy...

Dad had a choice going back. He could follow Upper Crab Creek to Tensas River and then head South on Tensas to the Causeway. That was not the way to go when it was rough. Especially, with a wife and five kids in the boat. The better choice was to leave Upper Crab and take Lower Crab Creek to Bay Delvan... and then it was a short hop over to the Causeway and Autrey's Camp.

He took Lower Crab Creek... but when we got to Bay Delvan it had turned into a pretty serious blow. He took the boat out of Crab to see how bad it was. Then quickly ducked back into Crab Creek.

Now, he had to make a choice... Risk it, or head back to the camp and go home tomorrow.

My Dad never missed work for any reason. He could have partied all day long with his Crewe of Columbus Mardi Gras group... rode in the parade and be solidly lit... but he would ALWAYS go to work. So going back to the camp was not a choice for him.

We had passed by a huge log up on the bank just at the end of Lower Crab Creek. He pulled the boat back up to it and decided to let me and Ricky stay on that log while he ran the others to the Causeway. Then he planned on coming back to get us... I was 11 and Ricky was 4...

The lower end of Lower Crab Creek is barely above water. The log we jumped out on was on the bank (See Fig.4), but water was already over the bank and about ankle deep... We were fine to stay there. We had grown up in the delta. Even at that age, we could handle standing on a log in the middle of the swamp for an hour... no big deal to us...

Dad and the rest take off for the causeway. I could see the boat hit Bay Delvan, the waves have now gotten pretty good, That Stauter is throwing white water off both sides... as it makes its way across Bay Delvan.

Me and Ricky sit on the log and kinda talk and entertain ourselves... My Dad and his brother Ralph had killed a big buck in that same location just a few years before. They rounded the corner as the deer jumped in the water. We had heard that story many times before. Ralph got so nervous that he could not shoot, so Dad did.

As we were waiting, I noticed the water was rising… No big deal we got this…

Just a bit later, I realized that the water was rising fast… The hard South wind and a coming high tide was pushing a lot of water up that creek… We still had it…

Eventually my Dad shows back up… it has been maybe a bit longer than an hour but not much. When he sees us standing about knee deep in water… on that log (Excuse me… I try to not cuss regularly, but sometimes it is required to tell a story properly) it scared the literal SHIT out of him.

He never told us how much it scared him that day. It took years for him to tell us… It shook him to his core, and he never forgot it. He would occasionally apologize to us through the years. We loved our Dad and knew he made the right choice that day… We had it….

Growing Up in Chickasaw and the Mobile Delta

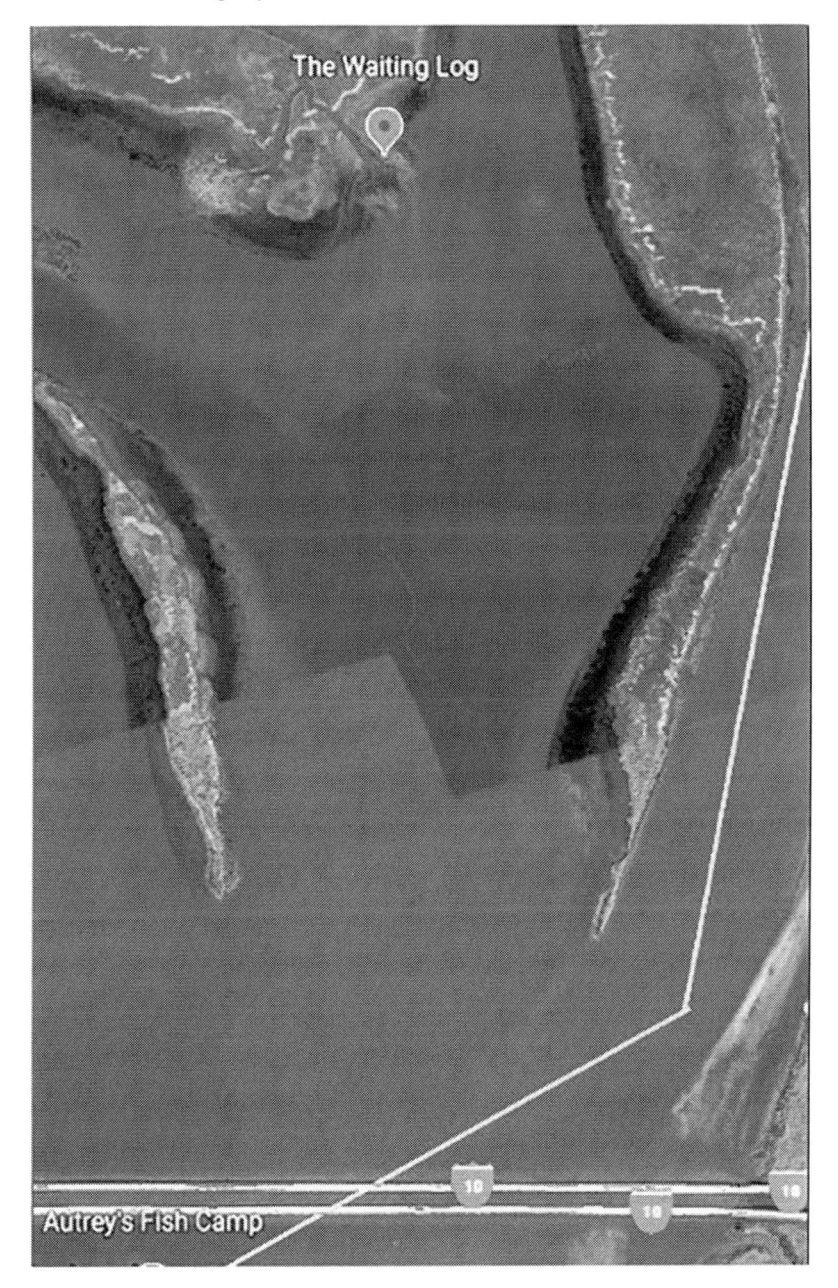

Figure 4

Ronnie Hyer/Vicki J. Barrett

The Gunshot...

I am sixteen years old, and the year is 1967. My dad will now let me take his Stauter boat with the 18HP Evinrude for a day of fishing, or just fun on the Delta. The boat is docked at Billy and Quennie Rice's Autry's Fish Camp on the Causeway. Me and my friend Leonard Nichols lower the boat into the water. It is held in the air by cables that wrap around a long pipe. Billy's design and it was a good one.

It is a Sunday. Warm day in late Summer early Fall as I remember it.

Me and Leonard head up into the Delta. Can't remember exactly what we did that day...but I will remember that day forever...

About that time of my life, I had discovered metal detecting. I usually spent every day that was not pouring rain and I had transportation... in the hills of Spanish Fort digging Civil War relics.

That day was probably spent doing something similar. About that same time, I had discovered history up in the delta. Both Leonard and I loved to find an old bottle on the bank of the rivers. We walked them a lot on low tides searching for anything over 100 years old. About noon we had decided to head back to the causeway for some reason. Probably the tide had come in... We head back down Upper Crab Creek and was going to hit Tensas and then to the causeway...

Now lets' stop for a moment... a few months before, I had bought a pistol from where I worked... Younce Hardware in Chickasaw. I do believe that every rightfully raised South Alabama boy wants to own a pistol at some time in his life. This was a 22 revolver. I used it on snakes, targets etc. Leonard is sitting on the front seat of that boat. I have the pistol in a holster on second seat. I am running that tiller operated 18 HP Evinrude on the back seat.

As we exited Upper Crab Creek (See Fig. 5) into Tensas the river had gotten a little rough... Things started bouncing around in the boat. The pistol in the holster is about to fall off the seat in front of me... I reach to grab it but could not quite reach it. I let go of the handle on the motor and just catch the pistol falling. In the flash of an eye that motor swings hard to the left or Port side... I try to stop it and.... POW !!!!!... the pistol goes off and hits me in my left leg. It happened so fast that Leonard did not even have time to turn around and look.

I get the motor stopped somehow. I have blood squirting everywhere. Leonard has no clue where we are... I HAVE to get us to the causeway...

I take off my shirt for a tourniquet and get Leonard to sit where he can keep it pressed on the wound... We take off for the Causeway.

About halfway there... Shock is taking over. I am losing a lot of blood... Everything starts turning blue and I can tell I am passing out...

Figure 5

My buddy Leonard is half sitting in the floor of the boat holding my wadded-up shirt tight to my leg trying to slow down the bleeding. We are trying to get back to Billy and Quennie's Autry's Fish Camp. Leonard cannot run the boat. It is getting rougher. I have to slow down a bit. We pass Conway's Creek on the left... Blood is now everywhere. I start feeling faint... I am anxiously trying to not pass out.

Suddenly.... just as I needed it... a cold rain hits us. It runs off the faintness and I am now good to go...

We get close to the Causeway and hang a right to enter Autry's Fish Camp. We need an ambulance desperately...!!

We pull in to the first set of stalls and go right to the wharf, where we usually load the boat. There are two cars backed up and they are loading a boat. It is a Sunday and Autry's is not usually very busy on a Sunday. I am so happy to see people that might be able to help us get an ambulance. Leonard cannot stop holding the shirt compress on my leg. It is probably the only thing stopping me from bleeding out...

We pull up the wharf and ask if they will call us an ambulance... They will not even turn around and look at us. I plead with them to "Please get me an ambulance".

Finally, the two guys loading the boat walk over and see the blood everywhere. They ask what happened...? I am now frantic... I tell them I shot myself with a pistol... They ask where is the pistol...?? I point out the pistol in the bottom of the boat... NOW...!!!

As God is my Witness...they then said. "We don't have time".

The women got in cars and drove off and the men got in the boat and left... They left two boys there on that wharf. One with a gunshot wound bleeding profusely...

Leonard and I were then all alone. He could not leave me. 30 minutes went by. The wound finally clotted, and as long as I did not move, the bleeding was stopped… 45 minutes went by, and nobody has stopped… Now it has been an hour wait… Finally, a guy walks up. We tell him what has happened. He runs off and less than 10 minutes later an ambulance arrives. They load me up and Leonard jumps in… It is about 1:30- 2:00. They take me to South Alabama Medical Center... and it is BUSY. People crowded in the Emergency. They roll me in… a quick examination and then they roll me down a hall. From then on, for the next several hours, I had to lay there perfectly still to stop the bleeding. A doctor or nurse would stop every now and then to lift my leg to see if the bullet came out the other side. I would tell them it did not come out, but every one of them considered it their responsibility to lift the leg and look. I would again lay perfectly still to get the bleeding stopped... that happened at least six times. As the day went on, I was highly entertained listening to the examinations going on in the rooms around me. One lady was being looked at because she had attempted suicide. They were going down the list of questions of what she had taken, how many etc, etc, etc… They got to the question of "When did you take the pills? Her answer was "Three Days Ago…!!" Exam was over and she was sent out of the hospital...!! I almost fell off the stretcher laughing…!!

Helicopter Crash…

When I was about 11 my Dad and I were headed up to his camp on Raft River. We had left Billy and Quennie Rice's Autrey's Fish Camp on the causeway. We went to Tensas, to Upper Crab Creek, and then up to Raft River. This was about the time my Dad, Melvin Hyer, was building his camp, but I do not remember what stage it was in. Dad was working at night then as a Pressman at the Mobile Press Register. He would get off work at about 4 in the morning, head home to get me, and we would head up the river to spend most of the day building the camp. He lived on very little sleep.

Sometimes we would stop by Ladd Supply to pick up whatever he needed. Lumber, Nails, Tar Paper etc... Sometimes we would stop by Gulfport Creosoting across from Scott Paper to pick up creosote posts. Those were the hard trips. Sitting on top of a dozen or so 10' creosote pilings in a Stauter boat headed up the river on a hot day has to be as close to Hell as anybody has ever been... here on earth. It burned your skin if you got any on you and it burned your eyes even if you did not.

This particular day, as we rode up the river there was about 6 huge helicopters transporting telephone poles into the middle of the delta. I remember asking Dad what they were doing. He told me they were building a practice helicopter landing pad in the middle of the Delta. I have no idea how he knew.

Each helicopter was carrying a huge bundle of telephone pole size pilings. I noticed that every helicopter was having problems with the poles swinging. I remember telling that to my Dad. He was running the boat, and in a hurry to get to work on the camp so he did not pay much attention...

As we exited Upper Crab into Raft River I watched as one of the helicopter's load of pilings swung way out one way, and then back in the other direction up to even with the chopper. As that happened, the helicopter and the poles (See Fig.6) fell out of the air... I hollered at Dad to look. He missed it but did realize that the helicopter he had seen a moment before was no longer there...

We got to the camp... I was still excited about what just happened and told Dad we needed to go look for them. He was not truly convinced that it had happened. I saw that the helicopter seemed to have crashed in the head of Oak Bayou...

About 30 minutes later the largest boat I have ever seen in the Delta, besides a Ghost Fleet Ship, came roaring up Raft River. It was a Coast Guard Cutter. It filled up Raft River and especially as he took a right to head to Oak Bayou... right in front of The Camp. He never let up on the throttle. The cutter threw a good 6 foot wave on us...!! Almost put that Stauter boat on top of the Wharf...

Dad was now convinced I had seen a helicopter crash. We jumped in the boat and followed them up Oak Bayou... The cutter continued on up Oak Bayou. We took a right to head up to Irving Lake. I think we use to call that Lewis's Bayou.

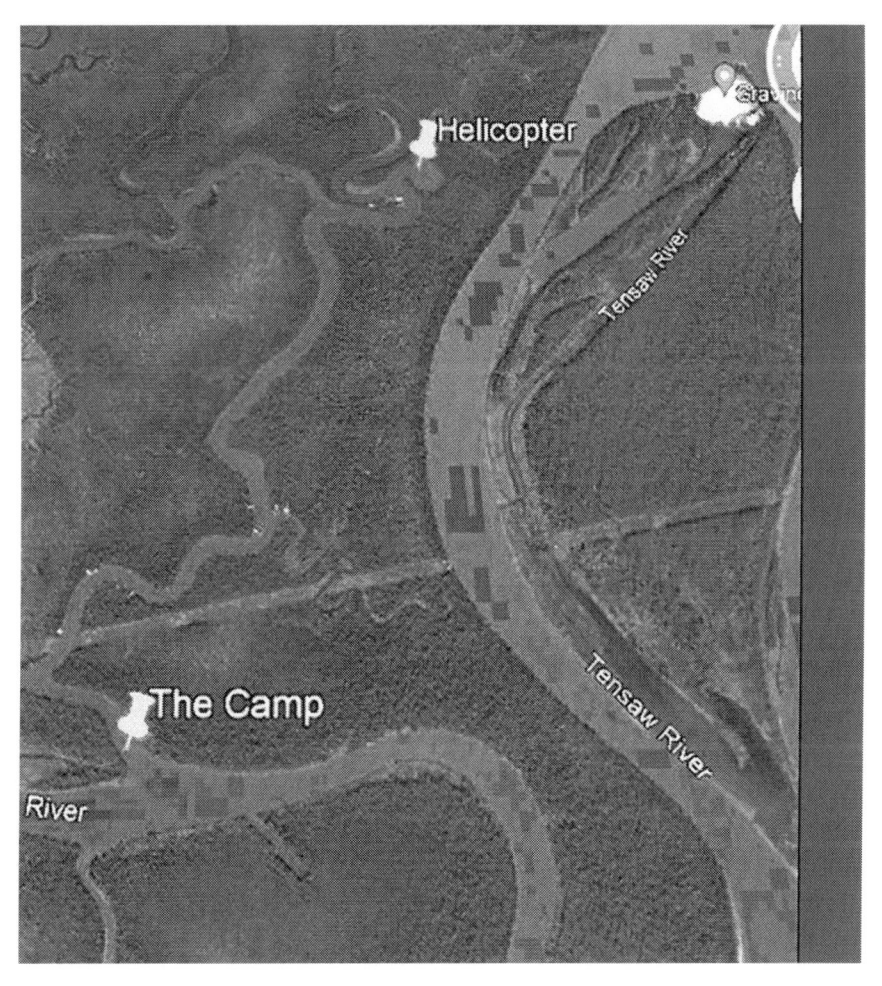

Figure 6

As we turned the corner there was the helicopter. The two guys from the chopper were floating around in a rubber raft... We let them know the cutter was nearby. They were a little shook, but fine. What impressed me most about the entire situation was how hot that helicopter engine and muffler was. It had already been an hour at least since the crash but that engine and muffler was still boiling the water like no tomorrow. Absolutely boiling like it had just hit at 10,000 degrees. I will never forget that one fact.

Once we knew they were alright we got the heck out of the way. I don't think that Cutter Captain has let off on that throttle yet. We did see them coming back out of Oak Bayou...at the same speed...

Quite an adventure for a young boy on what would have been just another forgotten day in The Delta in 1962....

The Oil Well…

Our camp was in the middle of the lower delta, and it always felt like we were a thousand miles away from civilization… Until they drilled that well…

We woke up one morning to huge barge loads of equipment parking on the riverbank across from the camp (See Fig.3). It was about 1964. Exciting for a young boy to watch. They started clearing an area of about 20 football fields. Then they brought in huge cranes and dug a giant canal to nowhere.

After all that, they started drilling… It went on night and day for months. Then it was over. Never found out if they struck or not.

Eventually, I figured out it was a wildcat rig searching for gas in that first Mobile Bay gas exploration push.

We were left with very deep blind canal with probably 12' banks from all the spoil to build it. It took many years for vegetation to grow back to hide the damage.

But thank GOD they never came back to look anymore…

Ronnie Hyer/Vicki J. Barrett

Treasure Hunting

I've been a treasure hunter and a history buff for as long as I can remember. The stories in this section are accounts of some of my adventures searching for Civil War relics from Chickasaw to Spanish Fort, Blakeley, and the Delta. Those were some exciting adventures that landed me in jail at one point. POLITICS!!!

Growing Up in Chickasaw and the Mobile Delta

Relics in Chickasaw...

I have loved history and searched for information and artifacts all my life... This is a tiny bit of information and the only information I know of on Civil War action in Chickasaw Alabama... my hometown...

Now are ya'll ready for another Chickasaw history lesson...?? You are...?? Well gather around and get comfortable as this one is going to take a bit... We are going back to the year 1865...

The Battle of Mobile Bay had been fought, Fort Gaines, Fort Morgan and Fort Powell had been taken... The Yankees controlled half of Mobile Bay... up to about Dog River and Fairhope. The Confederates "Us" were determined to hold Mobile.

The way to Mobile by ship back then was up Blakeley River to Raft River... Down Raft River to Spanish River... then Spanish River to Mobile River just above the Cochrane Bridge to come into the back side of Mobile... All river traffic had to take that route to get to Mobile. The West side of the bay was too shallow. To defend the water approach to Mobile we had set up a defense on the heights at Spanish Fort... on the Blakeley River. The Yankees decided to take Mobile... They marched 16,000 troops from Navy Cove at Fort Morgan who joined another 16,000 troops that were landed at Marlow Ferry on Fish

River... A total of 32,000 Yankees marched from that point towards Spanish Fort. The Yankees also had large ships sitting in the bay that could shell our Confederate positions in Spanish Fort... What type of defense could we muster up that late in the War...?? 1,300 old men and boys rounded up in Mobile stood at the ready... Our armies had been decimated...most soldiers were barefoot by that time and ammunition was short... Almost every single Confederate soldier that fought at Spanish Fort had already been shot at least once before... But once the shelling started and the bullets started flying our "men"... held off over 42,000 Yankees for 13 days...!!

As Spanish Fort fell, many of our men escaped through the swamps on a boardwalk that went from Apalachee River, out the back of Fort Tracey, and across to Conway's Creek. Ships picked them up there and carried them to Mobile. Many others of our men took another path through the swamp heading to Blakely where they also took part in that battle... After the fighting at both Spanish Fort and Blakely was over... the remnants of our army were in Mobile, and the Yankees were still on the eastern shore... They soon decided to come take Mobile. They landed all of their thousands of troops at Catfish Point on the Western shore of Mobile Bay... Where the Beachcomber Restaurant used to be... Now, of course, our Confederates still did not want to surrender. Some took river boats up the river to Demopolis... but most headed up the railroad tracks through Whistler... Whistler Station, as it was known at the time, was the home of very large railroad and machine shops... At Whistler the

Confederates decided to try to slow the Yankees down. The cavalry burned the railroad bridge at 8 Mile Creek and set up a battle line on the North side of the creek. Now here is where Chickasaw enters the picture... This was a huge number of Yankees chasing the remnants of the Confederate Army. The Yankees set up trench lines that extended from the turn on Thompson Boulevard in Chickasaw that leads to Whistler, and it went all the way to Highway 45... I have searched those trenches and located fired minie balls... in Chickasaw... and buttons and bullets all the way to Highway 45... The trench line in Chickasaw... if it still exists... was to the right, on the outside of the curve on Thompson Boulevard... and it ran down the hill towards Whistler... It could go on further... I never checked. Civil War cannonballs and shells were found just to the right as you come back up the hill into Whistler... As far as I know, that is the only real Civil War activity in Chickasaw. I was so amazed to find those minie balls 55 years ago now. I learned all this because I have done it all my life. We have searched for relics and artifacts throughout the South... but my favorite finds ever, were those minie balls found in my hometown... Chickasaw Alabama...

The Air Sho Treasures…

So, our business was located just on the other side of the Chickasaw City limits sign in Mobile… I am wanting to go metal detecting in the afternoon after work on those long summer afternoons… one day I drive by the old Air Sho Drive In and realize they have torn down the fence and removed everything from the site. I drive by it several days before I realize the potential… In 1964, the United States stopped minting silver coins. Those real silver coins were now worth much more than their face value. I had always been a relic hunter and considered coin hunters to be… well just not respectable… Phsaw…!! Real treasure hunters hunt for CIVIL WAR RELICS like me…!!

But I did need a place to keep in practice, so I stopped one day to try out the site… just for practice in case anybody asked… I kinda started at the admissions gate area and worked my way in. I was finding the odd coin or two, but that area was paved… so I was not expecting much. Worked my way up towards the front near the screen where the play area was, and… Bing…Bang…Boom… the metal detector was squealing louder than a bunch of Democrats after the last Presidential election…!! Targets were everywhere…!! Coins started popping up… Old coins… silver coins… I could literally stand in one spot and dig coins till it was time to leave. I did it for days and then weeks. It was amazing... Then it got even more amazing...I dug a Spanish Reale Coin from the early 1700's...!! I started finding very, very old coins... The Air Sho drive... How did these very old coins get there...?? It was built in 1955 and these coins are from 100, and more, years earlier...

My mind took me to the possibility of those coins being lost at that spot before the drive in was built and all other possibilities... it was a complete and total mystery to me until...

Several years later... after the finds... I was talking to a very serious coin collector. We were discussing the coins I had found in the past... Of course, this bunch of coins came up with the question how did they get there...???

With a twinkle in his eye, he asked me where I thought he had bought some of his best old coins...??

I gave him a very questioning look as my answer...

He said... "The Ice Cream Man".

It clicked, and all the parts of the puzzle came together...

Kids collect any coins they can find in the house when the ice cream truck came by... Everyone has a few old coins they have collected over the years... To a kid... all coins found in their parent's drawer are good for ice cream... AND, as I had now proven... for snacks and admission at the Air Sho Drive In...!!

Growing Up in Chickasaw and the Mobile Delta

Claurice and Wash...

Love to listen to and tell old stories... learned it from my Dad and all his friends at our fishing camp up on Raft River... on the island where Upper Crab Creek dumped into Raft... The men would sit around and tell stories after supper was over... It would last for a bit, and then they would get sleepy... Sometimes though, one of them would have stopped by Claurice's at Cloverleaf Landing and picked up a gallon of moonshine, or shinny as they called it... Then the tongues would get loose, and the stories would get loud and long....I loved it...!! I would lay there in a bed and just LMAO...!! My eventual Father-in-Law, Mr. Emmet Mulvey, was always there, and always had great stories... Mr. Billy Schemmer... Mr. J.C. Hudson... Mr. Nick Shamp... My grandfather, my Uncle Ralph, and Mr. Earl Stringfellow were all regulars... So many more that have escaped my memory 50 years later... What great times and memories to have.... It is a gift to be able to tell stories, and it was a great gift to be able to hear all those stories back then...

At age sixteen I became very interested in the Civil War history on the Delta. At that time, I was working at Younce Hardware in Chickasaw. Mr. Younce's daughter,

Jill, had started metal detecting in Spanish Fort and took me along one day. I was forever after hooked.

Soon got me a metal detector and have been searching for relics and treasure ever since…

At 16 years old, I was spending every moment I could in the woods of Spanish Fort and eventually the Blakeley Battlefield.

About a year later I found myself at Cloverleaf Landing now being run by Wash…. Claurice's son. Wash knew me, and we talked about My Grandpa and my Dad and his Dad and the old days. Wash called both my Dad and Grandpa Mr. Melvin because Dad was a Junior. Now Wash called me Mr. Ronnie… as had always been the custom in earlier times.

It got to be a routine. I would go metal detecting and always stop to talk to Wash and get me one of the coldest Coca Cola's around. Found a lot of great stuff around Cloverleaf Landing.

One day I woke up to a front-page story in the Mobile Press Register Newspaper. The story was about some guys finding and recovering a huge Civil War cannon from the bank of Blakeley River. It was a big article with pictures that told the story of how they found the cannon and recovered it. In that story they said that Wash had taken them to the cannon and located it for them with a fishing pole…!!

I was stunned. Here I have been going by and talking to Wash almost every weekend and he never mentioned a cannon.

Somehow, I felt betrayed. Why didn't Wash tell me about that cannon...? He knew what I was doing every week when I came by for a Coke and to talk...

A couple weekends later, I went metal detecting again and went by for that coldest Coca Cola in town and to see Wash.

We got to talking and I mentioned seeing the newspaper article. Wash started telling me how he knew it was there. Seems it was mounted on a barge that had been drug up on the bank of the Blakeley River after the Civil War. In the 1926 hurricane, that barge had floated a bit North from where it was sitting and turned over in the mouth of a little slough. The cannon came loose, and there it sat in the bottom of that slough until Wash went up there with those guys and found it for them with a fishing pole...

I was still somewhat shocked by missing such a huge opportunity to find an incredible Civil War relic... like a cannon... that it took me a bit to get around to asking Wash the big question... "Wash... you know what I am coming up here doing every weekend... How come you never told me about that cannon??" Wash looked at me and said, "Mr. Ronnie...you never asked."

I have never forgot that lesson that Wash taught me that day and it has been of great benefit to me later in life... Probably much more than had he showed me where that cannon was...

Thank you, Mr. Wash...

Ronnie Hyer/Vicki J. Barrett

A Cloverleaf Landing Story...

This is a tiny slice of Mobile Civil War Campaign History and a lot about me finding a Confederate Land Mine at Cloverleaf Landing or Claurice's as I had always known it...

Do you believe in Premonition.?

The year was 1968 and I was 17 years old. I had been introduced to metal detecting the year before. As soon as I could save up enough money... I had bought my own detector.

I was then in the woods at Spanish Fort every day that I could get there. Digging up Civil War relics became an all-consuming passion. I read everything I could about Spanish Fort and the Civil War. Some friends and I had even started a kind of Civil War reenactment group. We did not reenact any battles... We just put together what we could that looked like a Confederate uniform. Then we would go camp out in Spanish Fort and metal detect all weekend. Glorious fun weekends...!!

Mike Randall and Leonard Nichols and my brother Ricky were part of that very early group... The group was about 6-8 of us... Some interested in the Civil War. Some interested in metal detecting and some just interested in camping or just getting together...

Now the story...

I had borrowed a book from Jill Younce Breazeale on the Civil War. Jill Younce Breazeale eventually became Jill Armistead. Bill Armistead's wife... Bill was the fount of knowledge on Mobile Civil War information back in those days...

She had introduced me to the hobby. That book was not on Spanish Fort or Blakeley... it was on artillery shells. In that book, they described the first land mine ever used in combat… in the entire worlds history!! The first weapon in history designed to kill people that was not held or shot by another man... I read about it and filed it away in my memory.

I had no idea that the first time a land mine was used in battle was at the Spanish Fort and Blakeley Battlefield... It was just very interesting.

Keep in mind that at this time, I had never even been to the Blakely Battlefield. There was so much to find at Spanish Fort I figured why go further…??

But... the very next day after seeing a Civil War land mine for the first time in that book... for some reason, I decided to go to Blakeley... for the first time ever. I know Leonard Nichols, Mike Creel and my brother Ricky were with me and I don't remember who else. We drove down Highway 225 towards Blakeley. We were not exactly sure where to turn off... We missed the turn off to Blakeley Town.

We wound up at the Cloverleaf Landing Road. I turned there since I had been to Claurice's Camp that was down on the river at the end of that road.

We got to a dog leg in the road. I pulled over where people had been dumping trash as they always do in an out of site spot. We saw a trench running off to the South and decided to search it. Now... I had never before hunted the trenches. Everything in trenches was always very deep because time, rain and weather had washed all the dirt back down in the trench. But for some reason I started searching down that trench with the detector.

Maybe 50 foot along I got a nice deep signal... on the front of the trench.

WE started digging... About 18 inches down our shovel hit something metal.!! DING.!! We opened up the hole and could see we had hit something that looked like a brass pipe fitting... Gradually we worked it out... It was a perfect still loaded Confederate land mine...!! Invented in Mobile, Alabama. Probably made in Selma and sent to Mobile for the last large Civil War battle... One of the few that have ever been found.

Something led me to that exact spot...!! There were so many reasons I should not have been there...

Premonition...?? NO... something far beyond premonition... Something or somebody... meant for me to find that land mine.

Ronnie almost dies in Blakeley River...

So, it was a beautiful day in July... Actually, I do not know if it really was July or even if it was a beautiful day... but it WAS a day I do know that...

On this day, I had decided to go dive around Forts Huger and Tracy. I had been working those two sites for a while... maybe a couple years...??

When I first got to Fort Huger and Tracy (See Fig.7), I was probably the first person to ever search them with an underwater metal detector... The Forts themselves had been scoured by relic hunters before us with land metal detectors. I had been wanting to figure out how to search the water because I KNEW that a lot of shells and cannon balls were there.

I studied waterproof detector technology of that day and found the only one available was the Army Mine Detectors... They were huge things with a long heavy canister full of tube type electronics and huge heavy batteries... BUT it was WATERPROOF... I bought one at a local Army Navy Surplus Store... Back then there were real Army Navy Surplus Stores that sold real Army Navy Surplus stuff... Got it together... figured it out and got it working pretty well... Well at least as well as one of those machines worked. If you put it on a piece of metal, it

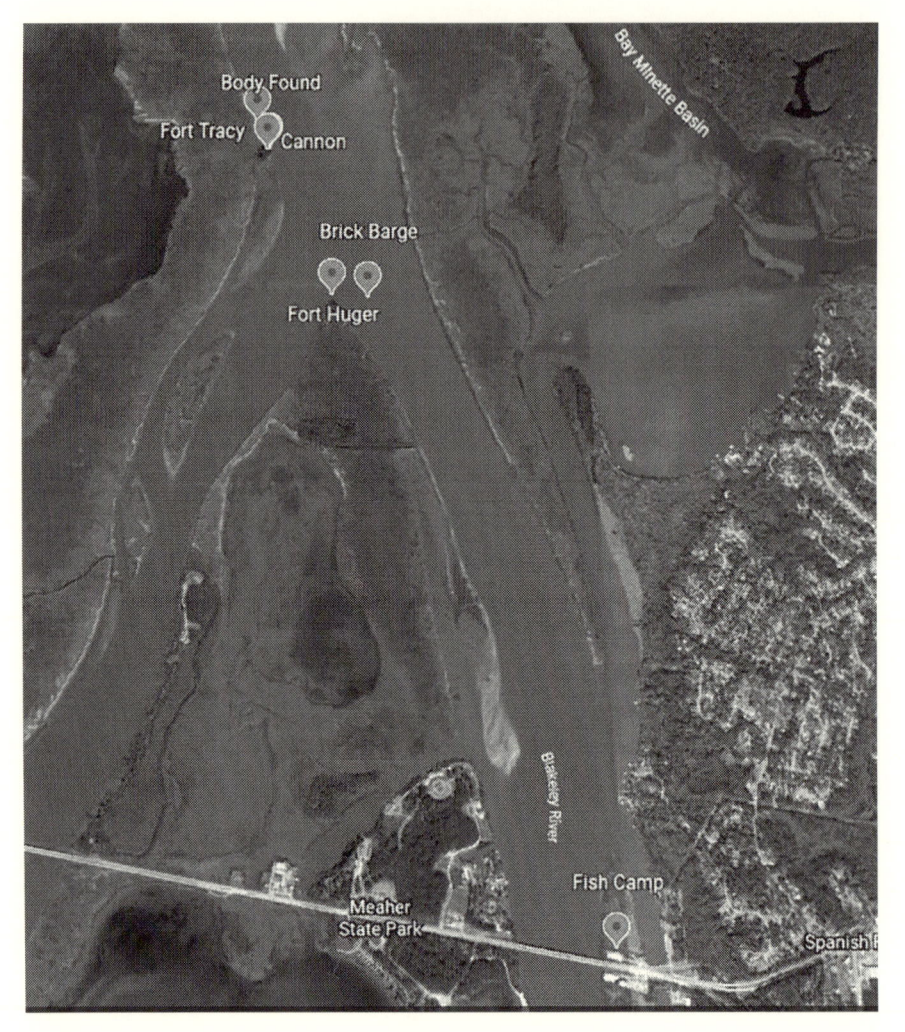

Figure 7

would tell you it was metal... and that was all the depth it had... But that was all we really needed...

The first day, I stepped off the bank at Fort Huger on the side facing Spanish Fort and into about waist deep water with that Army Surplus Metal Detector... we soon turned off the detector and put it back in the boat. We were stumbling over complete Civil War artillery shells... huge stands of grape and complete canister shot... the bottom was literally covered with every size grape shot, shrapnel and canister shot... the grape shot bases... the bolts and rings to hold them together... all of it was there... We picked up the complete ones and tossed the loose parts out into deeper water to get them out of the way...

Believe me... this story is leading to me almost dying there at Fort Huger. At the very least... me thinking I was going to die. I will get around to that. First you have to absorb some background information.

On one trip we filled that Stauter boat up with so many shells and cannon balls that I sunk the boat trying to get back to the Causeway. I was headed down the river and about halfway to the Causeway... the ass end of that Stauter boat started sinking... I made a hard right turn and ran it up on the mud bank... We dropped off some of the loot... bailed out the boat and took off again... We decided we should make two trips the next time.

Ronnie Hyer/Vicki J. Barrett

The Body...

I have been a relic hunter since 1967. I spent every weekend I could in the hills of Spanish Fort, the swamps of Blakeley, or somewhere in the Delta searching for history. For me it was an all-consuming hobby. There were no underwater or waterproof metal detectors back then. Today there are... I even owned a metal detector company based in Fairhope for a while. All we built were underwater detectors, but back then none were available. I happened to see a U.S army mine detector in an army navy store. It was a WWll/Korean War model. You carried it on your back just like you might have seen in the movies. It was not waterproof, but it had a long cable from the control box to the search coil. The search coil was waterproof. So, I had the idea we might be able to make it work in places never hunted before. I had, by then, heard about Fort Tracy and Fort Huger at the point of the Appalachee and the Blakeley Rivers.

One fine winter day, and when I knew the tide would be low... me and several running buddies took off from Billy and Quennie Rice's Autreys Fish Camp for the long run up the Tensas River and down the Blakeley River to the Appalachee. We were headed to Fort Tracy. When we got there, the tide was not yet low and high water was coming down the river from up above... There can be a wicked current at that point in those conditions. So rather than trying to park the boat tight on the point... we backed up the river just a bit so we could tie it to some willow trees growing on the back. We were going to jump out on the bank on the high ground where the actual fort was. Those willow trees were thick. We had to pull them apart to get close enough to jump to the riverbank. As we opened up those willow trees all of us saw something at the same time... It was a man that had drowned... He had on jeans and a winter coat and apparently had been in the water for a while. We were all still young boys, and the shock of this discovery affected us all... differently... We just needed to figure out what to do...

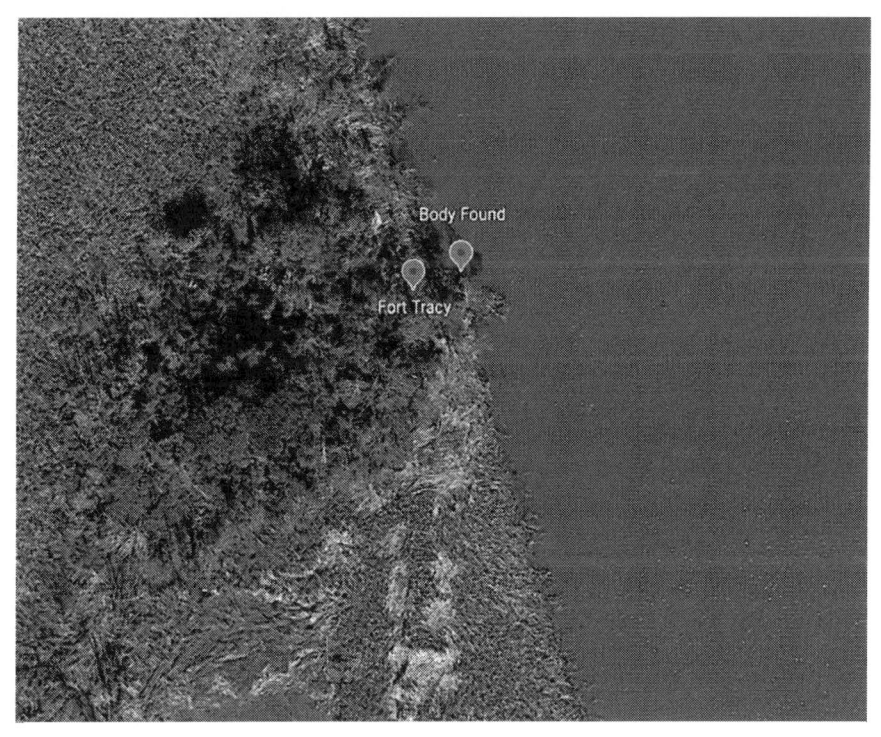

Figure 8

The man that had drowned (See Fig.8) came to the surface and got tangled up in those trees... 50 foot either way and we would have never seen him. After us boys got over the initial shock of finding a drowning victim, we started discussing what do we needed to do. I knew we needed to contact the Police and report it... The real question was where we needed to do that. Our options were Buzbees on Bay Minette Creek, back to Autreys, Claurice's (Clovise's) at Cloverleaf Landing, or straight to the Causeway to the camp at the bridge on Blakeley River. I had never been to that camp before, and it always seemed to be seldom operated. We decided on the Causeway... Young people... this was way back before cell phones. If you wanted to make a phone call, you better know where a pay phone was or somebody that would let you use their home or business phone. There was no other way that we were going to get in touch with anybody.

We chanced it on that camp at the bridge. Luckily somebody was there. We called the Sheriff's Office who said they were sending somebody... and for us to wait for them...
We piddled around... not much laughing or carrying on... It was as solemn as us group of boys had ever been, or ever been since... After a bit, a Sheriff car rolls in, and then an ambulance and one more car. They all got out and we told them what we had found and where...

We figured we had done all we could do and was thinking we were about to leave... The men had been talking among themselves and figured out they had no boat. They asked if we would mind taking them to the site. A young boy back then in South Alabama only knew one response to a Policeman. And that was "Yes Sir...!!" I told them that our boat was not going to hold all of them, my friends and a body... so what we gonna do? They said my friends could wait and that they would borrow a boat from the fish camp for the body.

Thought to myself... "Dangit... hoped to get out of seeing that body again..." But that was not to be... I was now fully into the body recovery business... They got a small rental boat with no motor and a rope. We tied it to the back of Stauter boat... everybody piled in to one boat or the other...and off we go... My friends stayed at the Fish Camp... I am now in the Stauter boat with three men and towing a small boat that has two more men that will be used to transport the body. At this point, I have decided that I did not want to get too heavily involved in whatever was coming. I did not mind giving men a ride, but I did prefer them to be breathing.

As we were headed back up the Blakeley River, the other men in the boat with me were talking among themselves. I tried to listen to what I could over the outboard, but they never even brought up one thing about the present situation. This was just another day at work for them. It was a long slow ride... almost like a funeral.

We finally get to the location. The men got out to go look at the body. I conveniently stayed in the boat. They pulled the small boat over close so they can work on getting him in that boat. First, they have to get him in a body bag, and then pick him up in the bag and into the boat.

Now stop for a second… at this point of this story… you have to make a decision. These memories are burned deep in my mind… but they do not have to be in yours… Stop reading now if, for any reason, you have trouble dealing with the harshest realities in life. I have not forgot one second of this even though I wish I could.

This man had been in the water for two weeks. It had taken that long for him to come up because the water was very cold. It was winter. Normally a body will come up in just a few days due to the belly and chest cavity filling with gases. In this situation, they badly needed to get a body bag on him before they tried lifting him in the boat. This man was a large man, but after being in water that long he has swollen to 3 times his normal size. I could hear them over there about 50 feet away struggling with the body bag and all of a sudden one guy says "The zipper just broke…!! "I think to myself "Not Good"…
Now they stop struggling and start talking.

Guy 1 "Have we got another bag"?
Guy 2 "Nope"
Guy1… What we gonna do…??

They turn and look at me...
Guy 1 "You got any rope?"
Me "Yep... the one you hauled that other boat up here with..."

They then decided that rather than calling for another body bag... they were going to tie the body in the broken zipper bag.

How did that come out...?? Not so good.

They cannot get the body bag fully around him, and even if they did, the rope was little help. But somehow, they got him in the boat we were going to haul back to the causeway.

The next problem was that we now had no rope to tie between the boats. The men decided that we could just hold the boat beside the Stauter boat and slowly make our way to the causeway. Here we go. Five full size men and me in the Stauter boat. The small boat is now overloaded with a body that is now mostly exposed... and we are doing about .5 miles an hour.

I am driving the boat. The motor is a tiller operated 18 horsepower Evinrude. I am sitting on the right side of the back seat. The boat we are holding on to is on the right side of the boat. All the men are sitting on the front two seats. We are headed South and there is a South wind. The smell of a decomposing human body is possibly the most offensive smell there is. It is unique and unforgettable. It somehow has a sweet horrifying element to it. I was sitting more behind the body and down wind, and I was catching the full brunt of the situation. The body was mostly uncovered, and the boat he was in was right beside me. I was also getting all the horror. His hand was right beside mine the whole trip. But his hand was massively swollen. It was a lot to take in at 16 years old…

I had to take myself out of the situation, so I started thinking about this man. Who was he? How did he get here? Did he have a family? After thinking for a spell... I decided I should be honored to be here. Somebody is sad and missing him. He did not mean to die, but it had happened. This man has lived, loved, and been loved by somebody, and here we are taking him on his last boat ride. Those thoughts made me feel a lot better. I grew up a lot that day back then… on that long sad trip.

We got him to the Causeway. There was some news media. I just wanted to get my buddies back in the boat and get the heck away. Nobody said Thank you. Nobody even noticed us… and that was just fine.

The next day after we found that body on Blakeley River at Fort Tracy… I found out who the victim was. His name was, Robert Brown, and was a friend of my Dad. One of his family members, and another friend of my Dad, Pappy Ray, called me to profusely thank us for finding Mr. Robert. Robert had somehow fallen out of his boat two weeks before. His boat was found in Tensaw River... two miles away from where we found him… It had floated that far as a strong storm had come up the night of the day he went missing... They were not looking for him on

Blakeley River at all... The family was desperate to find his body as he had left a wife and kids. He had life insurance that was going to help them out... but they had already been told that if the body is not found... they would have to wait 7 years to claim the money. They desperately needed that check. There is honestly not another reason in the world for a boat to stop there at the exact location... except the fact that there were a lot of people praying for that family, and I know in my heart that God had put me there... to help them.

The speculation at that time was that the storm, the night he was lost, had pushed his body up the Tensaw and then he floated back down Blakeley River to Fort Tracy... No amount of wind can make a body underwater move upstream. I have come to realize that Mr. Robert was somewhere near the junction of the Tensaw and Blakeley River when he fell in the water. His boat floated South on the Tensaw to where it was found. His body went down the Blakeley River to Fort Tracy at the mouth of the Apalachee River.

Recently, here in Fiji, there was a body found in a concealed wet area beside the road. I had been driving by that spot for over a week and knew there was a body close by. Once you have ever been exposed to a decomposing human body you never forget that smell.

I have been a very good substitute for a cadaver dog since this adventure at age 16. Now, at age 71, I have yet to out-grow that all-consuming adventurous spirit. In the intervening years I have lived at least ten lifetimes.

There is just a bit more to this story... That day actually ended on a very high note...

My buddies and I are now in the Stauter boat headed back up the river to Fort Tracy...

Yes, we are still on the hunt for treasure. In spite of all that has happened so far that day, there is still light. We still have that newly purchased WWll/Korean War surplus metal detector to try out, and there are Civil War relics yet to be found. If you go to Fort Tracy today, you will see a long sand bar that extends from the fort site South, and up the Apalachee River. Back in those days, that bar did not exist. I have highlighted the new sandbar in the picture.

During the Civil War Battle that took place at Spanish Fort, both Forts Huger and Fort Tracy were targeted by the Yankees. Those two forts blocked the only ship route to the City of Mobile. Before the battle, both forts were shelled by Yankee ships that were positioned just South of the current I-10 bridge on the Blakeley River. After Spanish Fort fell, the Yankees turned the captured Confederate cannons on Spanish Fort Hill on both Fort Huger and Tracy. The Yankees had gained nothing until they controlled Blakeley River. Both forts were massively bombarded.

Back on that particular day, nobody had ever used a metal detector out in the water just in front of Fort Tracy. We had chosen a day when the tide was way out, and it had been falling out more the entire day. The sandbar or flat in front of Tracy was completely exposed all the way out to the end of the old fort wharf. You could see every old piling from the wharf back then.

We set that mine detector up and started metal detecting. The very first target that made the detector sing... was a Yankee 30 Pound Parrot Cannon Projectile with intact pewter fuse (See Fig.9). It had been fired from Spanish Fort Hill at Fort Tracy... landed just short and failed to explode... it was just stuck nose first in that mud bank. As soon as the detector let me know there was metal there, I could see the base of the projectile. I simply reached down and pulled it out of the mud... It was like a payback for our good deed earlier that day. We were so dang excited.!! We had found an incredible piece of history, but more importantly, we had proven my theory that a waterproof metal detector could be very productive. People had already been scrambling over the land part of Fort Tracy searching with metal detectors for years. Here we have found a huge Yankee projectile six foot off the beach. We spent the rest of that day picking up a huge pile of Civil War artillery fragments. The whole sandbar was littered with iron.

And then we went home… We later talked about that day… About how we found all that stuff on the sandbar and how exciting it was. But we never once talked about finding and recovering that body. There are some experiences in life that you just tuck away… never to be discussed… until you write a story like this one. This was just one day in the life of an over-adventurous, young 16-year-old guy growing up in the Mobile Delta.

We continued to detect that entire mud flat off and on over the coming months. Again, it was covered with projectile fragments…grape and cannister shot of all sizes and other bits and pieces of metal from the construction of the fort and the battle that took place there… I am sure much was found after we gave up on Fort Tracy, as that metal detector had very little depth… but enough for us in those early days of our relic saving career.

One day we were there at Fort Tracy and a guy named Henry Davis who owned a dive shop in Montgomery back then… was diving off the end of the old fort wharf. They commenced to haul up a complete cannon carriage…!!! from just off the end of that wharf. That lit my fire…!! Now I knew I needed a better underwater metal detector and I needed to learn how to scuba dive... 6 months later I had solved both problems.

Figure 9

Ronnie Hyer/Vicki J. Barrett

Arrests at Fort Huger...

So Lamar and I researched and recovered all the Mobile area Civil War history that we could… as the years went by. We never sold one single relic… We collected them with the intention that all of it would stay in the Mobile area preserved and later… hopefully… displayed in a museum.

As the years went by, we observed the attitude of local Government and museums towards Civil War relics. We painfully watched the complete destruction of the Spanish Fort Battlefield by the Fuller Brothers who owned it. With no objections from anybody… We hunted the Blakeley Battlefield before it was closed and became a local country music concert arena… Nothing was done for years and years to preserve or even tell the story of what happened there… Now it is better. But we saw it being used for anything other than a memorial to our history.

I was there to observe a huge pile of Confederate shells uncovered on Davis Avenue in Downtown Mobile. The City took that pile of shells and piled them up behind the Mobile Museum and they all fell apart in about 3 years. Nothing was done and nobody even attempted to save any of those shells...

Back when the Fort Conde boondoggle was created... I was an office supply salesman working the downtown Mobile area... I was 23- 24 years old. Walked into a small office of an architect name Dewey Crowder.... Met a guy in the back working on what looked like a very interesting project. His name is Al Hunter... He showed me all the plans for the uniforms and all that was going to be at the new French Fort Conde. He told me it was going to be bid in about two weeks. I took a copy home and started making some phone calls... Two weeks later I won that bid for that project and over the next 18 months I set up everything at Fort Conde except the walls, floor, and ceilings...

It came time for the opening. I had supplied very, very nice and very expensive display cases for the museum area that they had... in the new Fort Conde.... Calls started being made for relics. People want to see what was found from the Fort or from that era... That is the MAIN attraction in any museum...

The proposed new City County Government Building preparations were also going on at this same time. They had hired archaeologists to come dig up and save all the historic relics before that building was started... It was not my responsibility, but I tried to find items for those museum cases at Fort Conde before the opening. Those archaeologists were contacted and would not give anything... or even loan anything. I later found out that all of the relics dug on the City County Building site were sold at the New Orleans Bottle show and other similar shows around the South... The small bit of items from that site on display in the front of that building today.?? is a damn joke compared to what was actually dug from that site. So, I gave up on that idea...

Next, I went to see the Director of the City of Mobile Museum... Same one that let all those Confederate shells from Davis Avenue fall apart earlier... I asked him in the name of the new French Fort Conde to loan them some relics to put on display... for the grand opening... his response was...

" I would not touch a CW relic or any relic with a ten-foot pole"...!!! It took me a very long time to digest what he had just told me. That is the reason Mobile has a very nice Mardi Gras/Black History Museum today...

So, with no other way to turn... the new French Fort Conde opened up with my personal relic collection as their display... And it stayed that way for several years. You see... back when they put the tunnel through and dug up the original Fort Conde site... This is years before the idea of a French Fort Conde... They dug up that fort site and hauled the dirt over town. They dumped it at Brookley... McDuffie Island and the Texas Street Park is almost 100% Fort Conde dirt. The approaches to the tunnel on both sides are from Fort Conde... Today... if you walk the interstate and watch for a gully formed after a good rain... you can still find buttons, coins and all types of relics from the original Fort Conde.

I was there at McDuffie Island trying to save all I could as it was unloaded and before it was pushed and crushed by the bulldozers. I saw the actual Fort Conde graveyard being dumped off the back of dump trucks... The large bones were still there... It was actual human bones and all parts of their uniforms... Myself and a very few more... saved what we could... Today, all of that is across the street from Frascati and under about 10-30 feet of fill..

After my collection at Fort Conde started getting stolen, I had to pull it out... But now... can you see my attitude on Government indifference towards our local history being formed...?? I am now getting the attitude that our history needs saving,.. not from relic hunters... but from the damn Government...!!!

This is just a question for you to ponder... The State of Alabama spent two years and a lot of money on an investigation and prosecuting me for recovering some incredible CW relics from Fort Huger... What do you think they did with those relics and where do you think they are today.?? Just a question for you to ponder. All of you arm chair historians that cheered when it happened… tell me where you think they are... Dozens of rare Confederate shells... a complete carpet bag... a complete wood case of 7.4 inch Brooke shells in the original shipping container marked Major Henry Myers Mobile Alabama... Dozens of Confederate cannon balls still attached to the wood sabot... all in picture perfect condition... Buttons... bullets by the score… Hand fulls of wood shell fuses... Bottles... a complete set of Confederate officers dining ware with pitchers and glasses... My personal book collection that was taken at the time of arrest to prove my ongoing criminal activity. Where do you think it is...??? Would you not like to see all that stuff after reading my story...??? Well, you can't, and you never will... but where do you think it wound up...??

Where is all that stuff today...?? Jack Friend made a huge deal in the Mobile Press Register newspaper about an initialed wood shovel handle... that I personally found... He declared that shovel handle an incredible relic lost forever to history... because we dug it up from the bottom of a river where it would have soon washed away... It was in a 5-gallon bucket water bath and would have been preserved as nicely as that wood cannon ball fuse I showed you earlier.... I KNOW how to preserve wood and all relics to last for generations to come... Only difference is... I do it for free and for the love of history... Archaeologists will only do it if they are getting paid... Jack Friend helped with the disposal of all those relics... because he paid the State of Alabama to prosecute me... the State was absolutely not interested and could not figure out if I had broken a law... Jack agreed to pay the salary of two Conservation Department officers for two years to get it started... I heard he spent $30,000.00...

Where is it all at now Jack..???... crickets... that is all you will ever get... even if you get close to the answer... That initialed wood shovel handle would be here today had over 50 cops not dumped all the water out of every preservation process I had going on. They took it all to Fort Morgan and dumped it out on the ground where it sat for weeks and months and then years... It is all gone... you can go see a few bottles which cannot be screwed up... but that is all that is left. The University of West

Florida came over and asked if they could have the unrecognizable lumps of iron that was left... about 2 years ago. They hauled it away...

Lamar Fox and I have now come to that time in our friendship where we know we will always be friends, but life has changed. I am running a fast-growing company and he has become the lead engineer at Alabama Power in charge of the Mobile District. We stay in touch... but we are not every weekend relic hunting buddies. But when something huge happens... we get in touch with each other.

Lamar calls me one day and says that he has seen an unbelievable pile of relics that I needed to see. We find a day to go to lunch together and he takes me by a guy's house. We go meet Larry McCoy. Larry takes me inside the house and tells the story.

But first, let me tell you about Larry... I had kinda sideways known Larry for years, He hung around the Confederate Ordnance Gun Shop in Mobile. Confederate Ordnance Gun Shop was absolute dead center for everything manly... guns... ammo... antiques... history and relics... in South Alabama. If you were a man or boy with any evidence of testosterone... back in those days... Confederate Ordnance was a regular required stop...

So, I kinda knew Larry from there...

Larry takes me inside his house and starts showing me scores of cannon balls and shells and... tells me exactly where he found them. Fort Huger...!! He describes how he was using a metal detector on the Apalachee River side of the fort and got a very low reading. He says he and a buddy dig down but could not get to the object... They figure out they needed to widen the hole because the sides kept caving in... Finally, the shovel hits something metal and out of the hole comes a 12-pound ball complete with the sabot help on by tin straps. He then pulls out that exact ball and shows it to me... He tells me that the tin straps looked like a new tin can the moment he brought it up out of the water. The sabot smelled like freshly cut pine wood.!! I am almost in orgasm... Wow what a find and what a story.!!

I am looking at dozens of that same type of cannonball... and dozens and dozens of shells spread all over his house...

Larry continues on to tell me that they dug that hole as wide as they could get it and kept finding shells but eventually, they could just not get anymore. The sides of the hole just caved in too fast...

My thoughts were "Who needed any more"...???

Lamar and I left Larry that day and later through the coming years talked about that experience we had... just seeing all that stuff Larry had found. Dreaming about what it must have been like to be there to see all that stuff coming out of the riverbank...but never even considered trying to go find it ourselves... Larry was lucky to hit that exact spot... we knew that... We also knew Larry would have never revealed the location had he not done everything physically possible to get it all... so we just dreamed on and continued living our lives......

So now... we are in the middle 80's... We are metal detecting when we can... thinking we are preserving history from the bulldozers and Government indifference...The ground penetrating radar (GPR) is providing some income from scans made for companies looking for underground storage tanks (UST)... I found UST everywhere... (under buildings... in the middle of streets in downtown Mobile etc etc etc etc.) and I have a gold mining dredge that I have some fun with occasionally... I have not mentioned it, but I was also involved with several unsolved murder mysteries and regularly assisted Police Departments searching for buried murder victims. The list of GPR adventures is long...

I was once paid to go to England to assist in the recovery of a 2000-year-old Viking treasure... I was at one time undercover in a Mississippi murder case involving the local police department... We could not let the local police know what we were looking for as they as teenagers were involved in or witness to this murder... As I said, the list is long... but this is about Fort Huger... so let's move it along...

In those mid 80's years I had seen those shells Larry McCoy had found... and I, later on, get a phone call from Larry McCoy...

Larry tells me that he knows a guy in Mississippi who has permission to dig a Confederate Cannon battery outside Vicksburg on Private Property that had blown up in the War... He explained that these guys have been digging for the shells that were driven underground in the explosion... have found a few but they think I might be able to help them.

They had no money but they were offering a share of the finds...

Hmmmm... I love the idea of an adventure like that..!! Hell Yes...!! I will go...

Larry McCoy was to get a share... for lining me up... Dan Patterson was to get a share as the Mississippi contact... and the guy who has the actual permission was to get a share. I give half my share to a buddy that is making the trip with me and will help me on the GPR... It is a two-man job

We take off to Mississippi. I meet the local guy, Dan Patterson and Larry McCoy... The day is rainy.

When we get there, I find out we have to carry my very heavy $30,000.00 GPR machine with a car battery to operate it... in the rain... about two miles into the woods... My equipment is not waterproof... but for God and the greater good... and the adventure, I decide to do it...

We reach the artillery site and I start scanning. It was clear that I was seeing large objects from 6 foot to 12 foot deep all over the site. I marked every large mass of those objects with a 1x3 post and orange flag... I put out about 30-40 flags.

Finally, it starts raining very hard... my work was done, and we head back to the trucks. There at the trucks it was agreed that the permission holder and Dan Patterson would be digging the signals I had located, and the share split would be honored. Remember my contact to these guys was solely through Larry McCoy...

Six months go by, I never hear anything... somehow on a day... and I cannot remember exactly where or how it happened... Larry gives me a single grape shot and declares "they never found anything but a few of these..."

I was not happy that all my work and risk destroying very expensive equipment... for that one nasty looking grape shot and "all they found".

Years go by... I become friends with Dan Patterson.. We are communicating regularly but somehow never discuss that search that day at the cannon battery...

But then one night on Facebook... I click on a picture of a huge pile of Confederate Shells found in Mississippi. The guy tells the story of a guy who came and GPR scanned a battery site for them and that they had dug this huge pile of Confederate Artillery right under the markers I had left...

I call the guy on the phone, he verifies the site and that it was me that had located all those shells. He even sends me a picture of 28 very Rare Confederate Read projectiles that he had dug from one hole. I ask him where all those shells went. He tells me that Dan Patterson had taken my share with him...

I call Dan Patterson... He tells me that he had sent "many" shells to Larry McCoy for me... for my share. Dan then sends me one of those rare read projectiles as I guess something to look at and continue to piss me off through the years...

Now... I did not go straight to Larry McCoy... I waited.

Larry has now gone into the gun shop business and succeeds in becoming famous. My ATF friends tell me what is going on... and that it is bad... very bad... I continue to wait... I have the inside track on the worst abuse of gun laws the area ATF office has ever seen... Karma is working.

One day, I was sitting with my wife in Steeles Restaurant in Bay Minette. Larry and his wife walks in...and sit nearby. I have since had my Fort Huger experience and Larry has spent quite a bit of time telling the world what a worthless P.O.S. I am... I couldn't care less but I was going to give him one more chance to lie to me... I walked up to their table not letting on that I knew why he was in Bay Minette... (Court)... Small talked for just a second and again asked him what they had found at that site I scanned way back up in the woods on that rainy day...back then...??

He loudly says, "he did not understand it"... "they never found anything...!!" I then let him know that Dan Patterson and I had become friends over the years and that I had talked to him and the other diggers and seen pictures of the huge piles of shells that were found. and asked, "where is mine?"... He turned his face to the window and would not speak. I left with a "Karma is Hell" ... There was no need to argue. I knew the shells had probably been sold to pay lawyers... so I marked that off as just a failed adventure...

I apologize again for the digression, but you need to know all the players... I am not perfectly innocent... I got "Gold Fever" that day after seeing all Larry McCoy had found at Huger and I wanted one... just one of those 20-pound cannon balls mounted on that pine wood sabot with those perfect tin straps. That was what got me there and we are about to take a boat ride...

Now we are back on track to get me arrested at Fort Huger. As I said earlier... I have a small 3" gold mining dredge and have been having limited success. I mainly used it as a digging tool while metal detecting out in the water about waist deep... Normally metal detecting in the water... you locate the metal on the bottom and then scoop it up with a metal scoop. The scoop looks like an upturned shovel with holes drilled in it... It has a handle that looks like a hoe handle, and we work out to chest deep water using this system. But I now have figured out how to drag the hose of the gold dredge beside me and use it to suck up targets a lot faster than a scoop... So, I decide to upgrade... I fly out to Keene Dredge in California and order me a larger 4" dredge.

The way a gold dredge works is the sand or gravel is sucked up in a hose and then run through a sluice box. The sluice box has riffles built into the bottom so the heavier items can drop behind the riffles in that slack current. That same concept is used from the smallest backpack style gold dredge to the largest barge mounted units you might see on Bering Sea Gold... I tried to use this new dredge in that normal set up... but Mobile Bay has a severe problem... From 100 miles above the causeway to the

Mouth of Mobile Bay... ANYWHERE you stick that gold mining hose on the bottom within that area... those riffles fill up with lead bird shot in no time at all. The entire bottom of the sluice box is solid with bird shot in an hour. The riffles are rendered useless... so you do not get to catch much of anything... I cannot imagine how much lead bird shot there is just in Mobile Bay, but I CAN tell you it is ENORMOUS...!! It took me a LONG time to figure out what was happening... but I did, and I modified the sluice box. I had no need to catch tiny items. We wanted to find lost coins... gold rings and maybe a few minie balls... So, I took out those riffles and drilled 1/2 holes on 1" centers all over that box. I tried it out in several places... It worked...!! We hit old swimming holes with good success finding rings and coins. I took it to my old hang out Johnsons Lake in 8 Mile and put it in the long-abandoned pool there... Found lots of rings deep in that sand bottom... Went to Ponchartrain Beach in New Orleans... also with good luck... Then one day in a moment of insanity, I started thinking about all those cannon balls and shells I had seen from Fort Huger... and started wondering what it might be like to find one...

So, we visit Fort Huger the first time with my gold mining dredge. Am I worried I am doing something wrong...?? Not at all...!! There are two fishermen in a boat nearby. I am worried about disturbing their fishing... but that is it... We have been coming to this same location to metal detect now for 15-20 years. We have watched it wash away over those years. Large trees are always in the water... after falling in from the eroding bank. We consider ourselves saving relics from forever being lost down the river…

The fishermen leave… we set up and start sifting sand… A gold mine dredge is not designed to remove sand or mud… it is strictly designed to lift it up… sift it… and drop it back in the water. A gold miner wants to find nuggets… we wanted to find relics.

We poked around all day… found maybe two minie balls…and then we left. We are now thinking nothing is there. Larry McCoy got it all back when he dug here back then… but we went back again several months later. Same result… not very encouraging at all…

Now… my wife…"at the time" owned a shop in Fairhope. She had a lady working for her and I met the lady's husband… In a conversation we were talking about my hobby……He made the worst decision he ever made in his life…!! BAR NONE…!!

You see this fine man was a deacon in the First Baptist Church… he sang in a Christian Quartet… he was a registered VERY successful engineer… These two people are a picture of everything good and holy about America… But in a split second he made that awful life changing decision to ask me…" Say that sounds like a lot of fun… I would like to go with you sometime"…

So, a few weeks later we go… Now we have been up there two times with almost no success… I KNOW where Larry found the shells… We have poked around up and down that shoreline. We spend this day doing almost the same thing with almost no results… At the end of the day

I declare it over and that this is the last time we are coming here... We are gathering up all of our equipment and suddenly it occurs to me that we have parked the boat in the exact same spot every time we came. I stop the guys and tell them to move the boat... we are going to make one last try under the spot the boat is parked in...

I stuck that nozzle in the sand... it went down about 18 inches, and I felt a "dink"... I reached my hand down in the hole... felt something round... pulled it up and there it was...!!!

A 20-pound Confederate Cannon Ball mounted on a pine sabot, the sabot smelt like fresh cut pine. the tin straps that attached the sabot to the ball were as shiny as a new tin can... We had hit the MOTHERLOAD right under where we had always parked the boat...!!

First try with the nozzle and I am now holding history in my hand... and then, it was one cannonball after another. We probably took home about 10 balls and a couple shells that day... We put them in the boat where they would not get damaged. Those pine sabots were waterlogged and were soft. We headed to the causeway and got it all home. Put it all in individual 5-gallon buckets of water to keep the oxygen away and to get them prepared for the preservation process. Of course, we went back the next weekend... This time we hit a pocket of material that was dry...!! First thing I noticed was Civil War Periods pontil bottles popping up to the surface full of air... They would just pop up and start floating away in the current. It is a LOT of fun chasing perfect 1865 CW pontil bottles down the river... Next thing that started popping to the surface was wood cannonball fuses. All of a sudden, all around me were perfectly dry floating wood cannonball fuses. They were also trying to float away in the current and now I am chasing fuses everywhere. Then... I was letting my new friend use the dredge and he hits something... It is about chest deep where he is... He dives under and comes back up to tell me it is a BOX...!! We use the dredge hose to free the box and dive under to get it out. It takes both of us to lift it even in the water. We get it to the boat and then on the boat... It is a perfect wood box. It is now covered with mud and my buddy takes some water and washes it off just a bit... Right on the top on the box is a black stencil that says, "Major Henry Myers Mobile Alabama" The top of the box is loose and we easily raise it to see what is inside. As we peered inside, we saw perfect 7.4-inch Brooke Projectiles and Canister shot. Major Henry Myers was the Confederate Quartermaster in Mobile at the time of the Spanish Fort and Blakeley battles. These shells had been shipped from Selma, Alabama to him in Mobile for use in those battles... and then were dumped in the river the night of the abandonment of Fort Huger...

Now, what do we do with all this stuff...?? We show EVERYBODY... We are not worried that we had done anything wrong... at all. We took a lot of it to show at our monthly metal detecting club meeting, and that was where trouble started... Relic hunting... treasure hunting... gold mining and fishing and hunting all inspire jealousy...

We went to that beach at Fort Huger three times successfully with the gold mining dredge. The final time there we found a beautiful crystal table pitcher... A carpet bag but the carpet had deteriorated... Lots of shells 100-pound Parrot shells and others... and then that was it... We decided that we had had a great time recovering what we found. We had years of preservation in front of us... We left that spot and never went back... Time went by... later I learned that a rat had been planted in the metal detecting club by Jack Friend. Jack got mad when he heard we found all that stuff... So mad he went to Montgomery and talked to everyone he could to try to get something done about it. No agency was interested. He finally agreed to pay two Conservation Officers salary for two years to investigate me.

So, two investigator goofs join the metal detector club and start attending meetings. Looking back now, it was a pretty hokey investigation... Had I of known at the time... or if anybody would have just asked what was going on... I would have told them everything. I had checked with everyone that I thought I needed to... to be sure what I was doing was legal. As it turned out... years later... Everything I did WAS legal... I just got jammed up in court with a "Let's Make a Deal" attorney and had watched my family suffer too long...

About a year later I got several phone calls... The first phone call was from a friend in the Alabama Bureau of Investigation. He let me know that an investigation was going on and that they had found nothing to arrest me for... but do not go back to Fort Huger. I was stunned...?? The next phone call I got was from a member of the Mobile Camera Club... He tells me that I am a part on an investigation and gives me copies of the pictures they had him develop…!! Wow…!! I am now getting a bit spooked… and of course we were not planning to go back to Fort Huger and we never did. The investigators were getting antsy… after a while… They knew what I had done… They could find no law I had violated but wanted to get me back up there to Fort Huger to arrest me for something… The two investigator goofs in the club start trying to buddy up with me. One asked me to go to Fort Huger to get some bricks for him so he could build a fireplace in his house. He wanted Fort Huger bricks he says… I think I could have come up with a better story that that… I blew him off like he had the COVID virus.

And about that time… I decide to start an underwater metal detector company… Search Scan… we were very successful very fast, and I am quite sure that fueled the flames of hatred for Ronnie Hyer in the armchair historians and Jack Friend's mind…

I am now aware that I have pissed off some people…but I am also aware that they have been trying to figure out if what I have done is illegal… for over a year… I was also told to just stay away from the site… No problem…!!

I was off doing other things… Still doing plenty of Ground Penetrating Radar jobs and I decided to start a metal detector manufacturing business. I first went to see the Compass Metal Detector Company to see if it was worth buying… It was not. Then I found two guys in Pompano Beach Florida building detectors, and I liked what I saw… I brought them up to Fairhope, Alabama and set up a manufacturing facility. Within 6 months we were well on our way. The largest detector distributor was selling our products and the largest metal detector dealer was promoting our machines.

About one year into it… I got a call from the Baldwin County Historical Society… They wanted to meet me and talk about Ground Penetrating Radar… I met with them at Tim Ford's house in Spanish Fort… They asked some questions about radar and could it find graves.?? I gave them the answer that of course it easily found graves and that I had located graves literally all over the South and in England by that time…

Well… then the leader of the group Davida Hastie tells me why they need me… She tells me that they now think they know where the mass grave is at the Fort Mims massacre site. The largest Indian massacre of white people in America…!! Which is just up the road in Baldwin County. She explains it is on property next to the Fort site. I tell her and the group… no problem… just get permission and I will be glad to go do it. She then explains that there was no way they will be able to get permission since they had already pissed off the property owners… I was wide eyed and asked…

'What do you want me to do…??

Without batting an eye she said… "We want you to go over there at night and find that grave… Once we know it is there, we can take the property away from them…" I was shocked at the incredible audacity of these people, and they had just met me…

I gave them no answer but since they now thought they had drawn me into their confidence...Davida Hastie asks. "Have you heard about all the relics that were found at Fort Huger...??" "Cases of Confederate Rifles and all kinds of stuff... "We are about to arrest the guy...!! "I said... Wow... and that was it... I left that meeting wondering what I had just been asked to do and by what kind of people... You see that is the mentality of the typical "armchair historian"... They think them and their cronies can do no wrong... but let a seriously interested person go out and actually save some history... and they are ready to crucify them... I went home shaking my head...

The actual arrest is just ahead... as predicted by Davida Hastie.

We are watching Ronnie walk out the door of a meeting with the Baldwin County Historical Society... where he has been propositioned to commit a crime in the name of "saving history"... and told he is soon to be arrested...

I did some checking... The investigators have now involved Baldwin County District Attorney David Whetstone... Mr. Whetstone had formerly been a local attorney in Gulf Shores that few knew... But David had connections in Montgomery. Our Baldwin County District Attorney assumed room temperature (died) and David spent no time crying about it... He took off to Montgomery as fast as he could get there... worked those connections and got himself appointed Baldwin County District Attorney...

Now two things you need to know about David Whetstone... Every case he tried was chosen to get himself reelected and he never saw a microphone or a camera he could pass up. Now the investigators have David pushing them for results because he smells a huge news story... but they still could not figure out what to arrest me for.

Time is coming to an end on the money given by Jack Friend for the investigation...

Me...?? Hell... I am out selling the crap out of metal detectors... We had developed two very nice underwater detectors. We were working with several different groups of treasure hunters working the Spanish Shipwrecks in South Florida and now had dealers all over the U.S. selling our products...

I decide to make a trip to see our dealers down through Florida and then have a three-day vacation in Key West... I left home and drove to Orlando to see Kellyco...the largest dealer of metal detectors in the world... I get to Kellyco and we spend about 3-4 hours talking... Before I left, they gave me a $30,000.00 order for detectors and paid me up front...!! I walked out their door with the largest order I ever imagined with cash in hand...

My next stop was to be Fort St. Pierce... A long drive... I called that dealer and told them I would be late coming in... They told me not to worry that they wanted to see me, so they were going to be waiting for me whatever time I got there... It was about a 5-hour drive... When I walked in their shop about about 9 PM.... I was looking at two very pale people. The only thing they could say was... "You need to call home!!"

To be honest, the next few minutes are now almost a blur... I called home and my Search Scan Factory Manager Howard answered the phone...

He said "Ronnie... I am at your house and there are at least 50 policemen tearing it apart.!!" I gulped and asked... "Which Police...??"

He said that they were from every department he has ever seen...!! A.B.I Conservation Department, Baldwin County Sheriff's Department and on and on and on and on...

I then asked Howard... "What are they looking for...??"

Howard told me that he had been handed a search warrant for Cannon Balls!! Of course, I was totally unnerved... Now imagine this... those two people I had come to see was standing there watching me get this information... They were also unnerved... and white as sheets...

I then asked them could I use their phone to call my lawyer in Mobile. I called my lawyer... when he heard me on the phone, he said... "Where are you at...??" I told him... he said to stay there for a few days... He then told me that the news story had hit all the TV channels at 6 PM. He told me that they were spending more time on my story than the Kennedy Assassination... He said they were doing 10-minute news segments...!!

I did as he told me... I headed further South into the Keys... found a hotel room and did not sleep one wink for three days...

All this time, the husband of the lady that worked for my wife...?? The guy who made the awful mistake of asking to go metal detecting with me...?? That absolute wonderful guy... Deacon in his Church... Sings in a Gospel Quartet... got his picture all over local and national news everywhere... I was scared to call anybody. I just laid in a bed in a hotel in the Keys... Thinking... no sleeping just thinking...

So now we have been arrested... I have a useless attorney in Baldwin County... the kind that likes to hear himself talk and charges you to listen. This is my first time ever needing a lawyer for anything like this... so I am oblivious as to what to expect...

I am still manufacturing and selling metal detectors but quickly losing interest. Wound up selling that company to a friend who continued forward with it...

The case was so shaky for the prosecution... they actually went to my hapless new buddy that got arrested at the same time... and offered him immunity to testify against me. I told him to take the deal... He knew nothing, and I had done nothing.

David Whetstone catches a break when two idiots trespassed into Blakeley Park at night in a stolen boat with a cheap detector and got caught. About two weeks after my arrest... He got several more days in front of cameras proudly proclaiming that he was the Savior of Civil War history...!!

Time drug along... they offered a deal. $30,000.00 fine... 2 weeks in jail and 2 years of probation... My do-nothing attorney got me to agree. I was sick of all of it... I was tired of all of it. I was just worn the hell out and wanted to get it over.

We went to court... I got there ready to take the deal. All of a sudden, David Whetstone gets so nervous that I might not plead guilty... he starts negotiating with himself... You see he has made a lot of promises and desperately wants to be the next State Attorney General. He thinks I am his ticket to that office. I am sitting there ready to see the judge in a few minutes and he starts sending messages to my worthless attorney.

He drops the two weeks to two days. Then he sends a message that he will drop the $30,000.00 to $13,000.00... I am shocked and should have realized what was happening... More importantly my DA high-paid worthless attorney should have realized what position I was in...

Next David Whetstone drops the charge to a misdemeanor trespassing into the public waters of the State of Alabama with a $1.00 fine. 100 hours of Public Service...$13.000.00 restitution, that I know went to Jack Friend, and 2 days in county jail... That left me with no record, and some minor inconveniences. I took that deal. Had I of waited 10 more minutes I would have also gotten rid of the inconveniences... but again my "let's make a deal" attorney was beside himself to "Make a Deal"...!!

After I took the deal... I had to go back to formally receive my agreed sentence. They canceled the date several times. When that day finally came, I realized why they kept canceling... David Whetstone had been trying to set up a huge Press Conference coinciding with my sentencing...

He did get maybe two nobodies to show up and after I got my sentence... David tried to stand up and make a speech in the courtroom. The judge told him to stop and that he was NOT going to do that in his courtroom...

We left... I did all I was supposed to do... Found one weekend when nothing was happening and went and checked myself into Baldwin County Jail for 48 hours... I checked into the trustee section... Bunch of nice guys... One guy's wife sent in a huge, delicious shrimp salad. I washed dishes two hours a day. All in all, a decent adventure... Did see one good fist fight right beside my bunk...

I went to the Conservation Department and lined up 100 hours at Gulf Shoes and was doing that... Jack Friend found out what I was doing and was pissed. He got Whetstone to demand that I go to Fort Morgan and dig up bricks out of the sand and stack them in the middle of the summer. I lasted about 3 hours... Went back to the judge and told him what was happening, and he stopped it immediately. I finished up identifying and cataloging fish pictures for the Conservation Department...

And that was it... I have since turned my life of crime around... Myself and Steve Phillips who also got arrested in the river at Selma spent a lot of time lobbying lawmakers in Montgomery. Today, what we were both arrested for...is legal. I got a letter from the State Attorney General's Office stating that the only protected items in the waters of Alabama are items attached to a shipwreck or underwater logs.

All of the relics we recovered were allowed to rust away or just fall apart at Fort Morgan by the Conservation Department, Baldwin County, and the Fort Morgan Museum staff...

That is the real tragedy in this story... I understand what I did and for what reasons... but why did The State of Alabama go to all that expense, manpower, and time just to let it be destroyed...??

That reminds me of the old saying or story that goes something like this.

"When everybody is responsible... nothing gets done."... and nothing got done.

Poisoning the Delta

When I was a kid, there was abundant wildlife and aquatic vegetation in rivers around Mobile and the Delta. Many sad changes were occurring then, and still continue to occur. Wake up folks! Industry has poisoned our paradise!

Ronnie Hyer/Vicki J. Barrett

Sad Changes in the Delta…

Sometimes every now and then I get in the story telling mode… ya'll please forgive me for being so verbose. I got short time left now and a lot of stories to share…

The Mobile River Delta was once a haven for wildlife. When I was a kid we would duck hunt in Grand Bay, Chuckfee Bay, Little Bay John and all over that area. When you ran your boat into Grand Bay or Chuckfee a thousand ducks would get up in the air. In my youngest days there might be two other boats hunting either Bay…

My Dad and Grandfather remembered the days long before I was born. They said the sky would go dark when the ducks got up. My grandfather was one heck of a shot. He was also a functioning alcoholic… Grandpa would wake up to go duck hunting and down a pint of whiskey before his feet hit the floor. Just to warm up a bit. He loved to shoot Teal. The fastest and hardest to hit duck in the delta. Everybody would talk about how he would shoot one box of shells and bring home 20 plus Teal… He loved to shoot doubles. Few others even tried.

Over the years more hunters showed up… The limits got put into place, the ducks got scarce and my Grandpa grew old… We stopped duck hunting.

What happened to the ducks? At that time people blamed the hunters in North Alabama for putting out huge heaps of corn and stopping them short of us further South. That was not the reason. Others blamed the increase in hunters… It was hard to even find a spot to put a blind. That was not it either.

During those same years, one by one, chemical plants were being built for 60 miles North of the Delta… Each plant added a huge load of pesticide or herbicide to the rivers. When we duck hunted back then there was grass covering the bottoms of all those bays. There were buggy whips everywhere. There were snails at the bottom of those buggy whips and dragon flies everywhere all over them.

You cannot now find any of that grass or buggy whips anywhere.

My Dad also worked for Ciba Geigy who made Diazanon a pesticide. Ciba Geigy had, and probably still has, a 36" pipe that empties out in the middle of the river. He ran the packaging operations. That facility he worked in got covered in Diazanon dust in daily operations. They would wait for a huge rainstorm to make the river rise… and then they would wash down the whole plant letting all that Pesticide run out that 36" pipe in the middle of the river.

We also used to run catfish nets. When the river would rise Monsanto or Stauffer Chemicals would also wash their plant down and into the middle of the river. Their product was a little easier to see. Nylon would plug our nets up 60 miles below their plant. Every plant did it… We watched the delta die as far as we were concerned…

No…. hunters did not stop the ducks or kill them all. There was simply nothing any longer in the delta for them to eat. So, no reason to come down or stop…

I lost both of my kidneys about 15-16 years ago to membranoproliferative glomerulonephritis. The doctors could never tell me why I got kidney disease but based on my history of eating out of the Mobile River Delta all of my life… especially in my younger years… you might just take a guess what happened.

The wildlife and the delta were, and remain, contaminated we know that. The ducks left, the Bays and rivers are totally denuded of vegetation underwater. Fishing will never even be close to what it once was… We have lost that forever…

But also…

The Mobile South Baldwin County area has the highest rate of kidney disease in the United States.

It has cost us a lot more than any modern benefits chemicals has given us.

If I could take you back to those days my Grandpa remembered… those days my Dad remembered, or even those days I remember… most of you would never want to come back.

Ronnie Hyer/Vicki J. Barrett

Polecat Bay...

Most of you do not remember Polecat Bay... but your Dad's and Grandfather's did. Polecat Bay was the most prolific area of the causeway. It had deep water that held fish and ducks and was fondly remembered by my Father and Grandfather. What happened to Polecat Bay?

"Polecat Bay was by far the most beautiful portion of our Causeway at one time. It was very deep and provided excellent fishing, hunting and home sites... the founder of the town of Blakeley had a farm there in the very, very early 1800's.

Some have suggested the demise of Polecat Bay was dredging spoil. That is totally incorrect... The only reason to dredge in that area would be to deepen the Mobile River Channel and Polecat Bay is simply too far away to pump dredge spoil.

Alcoa Aluminum set up a plant around World War II and diked in the Western Shore of Polecat Bay to pump their waste.

That Alcoa Aluminum plant waste dump is what filled Polecat Bay... They put up those dikes around the once Western Shoreline of Polecat Bay... They then pumped that waste inside those dikes... They did it for years, but the diked area never filled up? Why.?? Because it was like a bowl of jello. They poured it in the top and it ran out under the bottom into Polecat Bay. That waste is dirt from South Africa that has been treated with strong chemicals to remove the alumina. Any of you remember that orange color??

"In the Bayer process, bauxite is mixed with caustic soda, or sodium hydroxide, and heated under pressure. The sodium hydroxide dissolves the aluminum oxide, forming sodium aluminate. The iron oxide remains solid and is separated by filtration. Finally, aluminum hydroxide introduced to the liquid sodium aluminate causes aluminum oxide to precipitate or come out of solution as a solid. These crystals are washed and heated to get rid of the water. The result is pure aluminum oxide, a fine white powder also known as alumina.

Why was it not stopped when it became apparent that the waste was spoiling Mobile Bay.??

Number One… nobody cared about that area. The few hunters and fishermen that did… still had excellent prime areas to move to nearby.

Number Two… for years Alcoa was the highest paying jobs in Mobile.

Bibliography

Personal Correspondence
Charles J. Torrey II, Research Historian, City of Mobile Museum

Books
Dejean, Joan, *Mutinous Women*, New York: Basic Books, 2022, p. 215-242

Raines, Ben, *Saving America's Amazon*, Montgomery: NewSouth Books, 2020

Websites
City of Chickasaw official website, cityofchickasaw.org

Wikipedia, en.wikipedia.org/wiki/Chickasaw,_Alabama

Photographs
Cover Photo of Chickasabogue, Leeann Hyer

About the Author Photo, Leeann Hyer

Made in the USA
Columbia, SC
26 September 2023

832d81c2-6873-48e8-97ca-8c9083e957f7R02